WITHDRAWN

CREATIVITY

contributors

JACOB BRONOWSKI
DONALD W. MacKINNON
WILLARD F. LIBBY
WILLIAM ARROWSMITH
GORDON PARKS

Creativity

A DISCUSSION AT THE NOBEL CONFERENCE
organized by Gustavus Adolphus College, St. Peter, Minnesota, 1970

edited by

JOHN D. ROSLANSKY

Woods Hole, Massachusetts

Columbia College Library
Columbia, Missouri

1970
NORTH-HOLLAND PUBLISHING COMPANY AMSTERDAM • LONDON
FLEET ACADEMIC EDITIONS, INC., NEW YORK

© 1970 – NORTH-HOLLAND PUBLISHING COMPANY

All rights reserved. No part of this publication may be reproduced, stored in a retrieval system, or transmitted, in any form or by any means, electronic, mechanical, photocopying, recording or otherwise, without the prior permission of the copyright owner.

Library of Congress Catalog Card Number: 74-134 641
ISBN North-Holland: 0 7204 4077 7
ISBN Fleet Academic: 8303 0111 9

PUBLISHED BY:
NORTH-HOLLAND PUBLISHING COMPANY – AMSTERDAM

SOLE DISTRIBUTORS FOR THE U.S.A. AND CANADA:
FLEET ACADEMIC EDITIONS, INC.
156 FIFTH AVENUE
NEW YORK CITY, 10010

PRINTED IN THE NETHERLANDS

Contents

Editor's acknowledgement	VI
Tribute to Sir William Ramsay	IX

The creative process — 1
JACOB BRONOWSKI
Salk Institute for Biological Studies, San Diego, California

Creativity: A multi-faceted phenomenon — 17
DONALD MacKINNON
Institute of Personality Assessment and Research, University of California at Berkeley

Creativity in science — 33
WILLARD F. LIBBY
University of California at Los Angeles

The creative university — 53
WILLIAM ARROWSMITH
University of Texas, Austin

Creativity to me — 79
GORDON PARKS
White Plains, New York

Editor's Acknowledgement

Those who were privileged to participate in this sixth Nobel Conference presented January 7 and 8, 1970; unexpectedly witnessed the magnanimous conduct of a college in the face of a tragic fire which destroyed the historic auditorium containing their administrative offices. With lectures, manuscripts, records, irreplaceable memorabila steeped in smoke and ashes; temporary quarters were already in evidence the morning of Jan. 8, becoming significantly functional the same day due to the heroic efforts of many. A business as usual attitude prevailed without interruption of the conference.
Particular credit must be extended to the student body for its inspirational conduct culminating in the form of a 'write-in' demonstration to assist in solicitation of funds for partial recovery of fire loss. Love must be learned in youth, lest it slip through the frail fingers of time. Participating symposiasts representing a spectrum of academic and non-academic careers were demonstrably touched by the decorum of the college family in the face of such personal tragedy. President Frank R. Barth reflecting the courage of his able staff during his introduction to the conference will probably prefer them to be less spectacular in certain ways in the future.

Credits for the repeat of substantial support by the Arnold Ryden Foundation, Tozer Foundation, Bremer Foundation, and the Board of College Education and Church Vocations of the Lutheran Church of America are respectfully tendered. Their continuing generosity reflects an expression of gratitude to the Hill Family Foundation for its original gifts which served to found this conference series.

Editor's Acknowledgement

A special word of gratitude is extended to Astronaut Colonel Edwin Aldrin for his considerations and it is regretful that he was unable to attend; Professor Neil Bartlett of the University of California, Berkeley, who has kindly provided the tribute to the memory of Laureate Sir William Ramsay at the recommendation of Dr. Theodore Shedlovsky, Rockefeller University; and Sir Ronald Nyholm for the accompanying photograph. It is the editor's privilege to acknowledge the many considerations of the college and the symposiasts extended to him and his wife which has served to make ours a most rewarding experience.

JOHN D. ROSLANSKY

Tribute to Sir William Ramsay

This sixth volume of the Nobel Conference Lectures at Gustavus Adolphus College, honors the memory of William Ramsay, winner of the 1904 Nobel Prize in Chemistry.

Ramsay was a giant in that age of giants when science was venturing out of the atomic and into sub-atomic territory. In the period 1894–98 Ramsay discovered a whole family of new elements, unsuspected even though The Periodic Law, established by Mendeliev some twenty-five years before, held a natural place for them. This sequence of discoveries followed from a joint research with Lord Rayleigh in 1894, in which Ramsay, a chemist, had joined forces with the physicist to solve a finding of the latter, that 'nitrogen' obtained from air, was denser than chemical nitrogen. Their solution was the discovery of a new element – the gas argon. This discovery astounded the scientific world (Mendeliev refused to believe in argon and preferred to think that the new gas was a new form of nitrogen, N_3!). Within weeks of the argon discovery, and by a typical piece of imaginative reasoning, Ramsay had discovered helium and thereafter, in a systematic and fearless progress, developed and established an hypothesis that argon and helium represented a new group of elements in the Periodic Classification. Argon and helium (the most abundant of the new elements) were thoroughly studied for chemical activity and were found to be chemically inert. The monatomicity and chemical 'inertness' (related features) of the elements were to play an important, even dominant role in the development of theories of the chemical bond. However, the discovery of the gases also had major influence on the development of theories of atomic structure.

Of course, the late 1890's also saw the discovery of radioactivity and Ramsay quickly got involved, when it became apparent that at least some of the new gases were also evolved from radioactive materials. With Frederick Soddy he established (1904) that helium was a product of the radioactive decay of radon (derived from radium). In this work Soddy and Ramsay were the first to establish that one element could change into another – they had witnessed a *transmutation* of elements! Incidentally, this discovery also gave immediate support to Rutherford's theory of atomic disintegration.

It is typical of Ramsay's deep humanity, that soon after taking up the investigation of radioactive change, he undertook, with several eminent members of the medical profession, a study of the curative action of radioactive substances in malignant disease, and unselfishly devoted considerable time and effort to it. He had a true pioneering spirit.

Born (1852) a Scot, he received his early scientific training in The University of Glasgow and took a doctorate in Tübingen (under Fittig) before returning to a university post in Glasgow, where he quickly devoted himself to physical chemical pursuits. He progressed from the Chair of Chemistry at University College Bristol (1880), to Principal of that College (1881), to the Chair of Chemistry at University College London (1887) where he was to remain until his retirement (1914). It is clear that Ramsay was the essence of originality. Apparently he was without any established belief in scientific doctrine and this made him incomprehensible to some. Above all, he was imaginative and enthusiastic and on several occasions he announced startling 'new findings' before they had been properly checked – it seems that, eventually, his 'group' saw to it that at least one junior colleague acted as devil's advocate to curb this over-enthusiasm!

It is not surprising that Ramsay had instant popularity with students and colleagues alike, and all accounts of him speak of his gift for friendship, it even being stated that Ramsay derived his greatest happiness from friendship. That friendship circled the globe. He was genial, approachable and great.

Shortly after his death (1916), his friends set up a fund to provide fellowships to support students engaged in Research in British Universities. As might be expected, the response was generous. Many British and non-British scientists have benefited from the free-ranging inquiry that the Ramsay Memorial Fellowships have given them – certainly Ramsay could have had no more fitting memorial.

NEIL BARTLETT
University of California at Berkeley

JACOB BRONOWSKI

The creative process

DR. BRONOWSKI *is a mathematician by training and, in addition, is well known for work in literature, intellectual history, and the philosophy of science. He works at the Salk Institute on human specificity: the analysis of those functions which characterize man and make him unique among animal species.*

Born in Poland, Dr. Bronowski was educated first in Germany and then in English schools and the University of Cambridge. He received his Ph.D. degree there in 1933. From 1934 to 1942, he was Senior Lecturer at the University of Hull.

During World War II, he was head of a number of statistical units studying the industrial and economic effects of bombing. In 1945, he wrote the British report on 'The Effects of the Atomic Bombs at Hiroshima and Nagasaki.'

From that date until 1963, Dr. Bronowski took a leading part in applying scientific methods to the economic development of industry in Great Britain. During this time, Dr. Bronowski was invited by M.I.T. to initiate a pioneer study of the ethics of science as the Carnegie Visiting professor. His series of lectures there on Science and Human Values became famous in his book of the same title. This led to other books on intellectual history and literary criticism.

His book The Face of Violence won the Italia Prize for the best dramatic work in Europe in 1950–1951. The book presents an analysis of 'the motives and manifestations of violence in modern society'.

Dr. Bronowski's combination of scientific and literary interests establish him as a leader in the modern movement of scientific humanism. Dr. Salk describes him as 'one of an increasing number of scientists who have turned their minds to thoughts about man.'

Since I am a mathematician most of what I write will, in the nature of things, be concerned with the problems of creative thought in science. Nevertheless, I want at least to glance at creation in the arts also: that is, at problems in the realm of aesthetics. I should therefore begin by saying that I do not regard aesthetics as a remote and abstract interest. My approach to aesthetics as much as to scientific thought is not contemplative but active. I do not ask, 'What is beauty?' or even, 'How do we judge what is beautiful?' I ask as simply as I can, 'What prompts men to make something which seems beautiful, to them or to others?'

This is a rational question and it deserves a rational answer. We must not retreat from it into vague intuitions, or side-step it with hymns of praise to the mystical nature of beauty. I am not talking about mystics: I am talking about human beings who make things to use and to see. A rational aesthetic must start from the conviction that art (and science too) is a normal activity of human life.

All the way back to the cave paintings and the invention of the first stone tools, what moved men either to paint or to invent was an everyday impulse. But it was an impulse in the everyday of men, not of animals. Whether we search for the beginnings either of art or of science, we have to go to those faculties which are human and not animal faculties. Something happens on the tree of evolution between the big apes and ourselves which is bound up with the development of personality; and once our branch has sprung out, Raphael and Humphry Davy lie furled in the human beginning like the leaves in the bud. What the painter and the inventor were doing, right back in the cave, was unfolding the gift of intelligent action.

If I am to ask you to study this gift, I must point to some distinction between animal behavior and human behavior. One characteristic of animal behavior is that it is dominated by the physical presence of what the animal wants or fears. The mouse is dominated by the cat, the rabbit by the stoat; and equally, the hungry animal is dominated by the sight and smell of food, or of a mate, which make him blind to everything else present. A mastiff with food just outside his cage cannot tear himself away from the bars; the food fixes him, physically, by its closeness. Move the food a few feet away from the cage, and he feels released; he remembers that there is a door at the back of the cage, and now that he can take his eyes off the food, away he races through the door and around to the front.

This and many other experiments make plain the compulsions which hold an animal. Even outside the clockwork of his instinctive actions, his needs fix and drive him so that he has no room for manoeuver. A main handicap in this, of course, is that the animal lacks any apparatus, such as human speech, by which he can bring to mind what is not present. Without speech, without a familiar symbolism, how can the mastiff's mind attend to the door behind him? His attention is free, his intelligence can manoeuver, only within the few feet in which the food is not too close to the cage and is yet within range of sight or smell.

Man has freed himself from this dominance in two steps. First, he can remember what is out of sight. The apparatus of speech allows him to recall what is absent, and to put it beside what is present; his field of action is larger because his mind holds more choices side by side. And second, the practice of speech allows man to become familiar with the absent situation, to handle and to explore it, and so at last to become agile in it and control it. To my mind, the cave painting as much as the chipped flint tool is an attempt to control the absent environment, and

The creative process

both are created in the same temper; they are exercises in freeing man from the mechanical drives of nature.

In these words, I have put the central concept of my aesthetic: evolution has had, for man, the direction of liberty. Of course, men do at times act from necessity, as animals do. But we know them to be men when their actions have an untroubled liberty; when children play, when the young find a pleasure in abstract thought, when in maturity we weigh and choose between two ambitions. These are the human acts, and they are beautiful as a painting or an invention is beautiful, because the mind in them is free and exuberant. And you will now see why I framed my opening question so oddly; for it is not the thing done or made which is beautiful, but the doing. If we appreciate the thing, it is because we relive the heady freedom of making it. Beauty is the by-product of interest and pleasure in the choice of action.

Now I turn our attention to action in the field of science. The most remarkable discovery made by scientists is science itself. The discovery must be compared in importance with the invention of cave-painting and of writing. Like these earlier human creations, science is an attempt to control our surroundings by entering into them and understanding them from inside. And like them, science has surely made a critical step in human development which cannot be reversed. We cannot conceive a future society without science.

I have used three words to describe these far-reaching changes: discovery, invention, and creation. There are contexts in which one of these words is more appropriate than the others. Christopher Columbus discovered the West Indies, and Alexander Graham Bell invented the telephone. We do not call their achievements creations because they are not personal enough. The West Indies were there all the time; and as for the telephone, we feel that Bell's ingenious thought was somehow not fundamental. The groundwork was there, and if not Bell then someone else would have stumbled on the telephone as casually as on the West Indies.

By contrast, we feel that *Othello* is genuinely a creation. This is not because *Othello* came out of a clear sky; it did not. There were Elizabethan dramatists before Shakespeare, and without them he could not have written as he did. Yet within their tradition *Othello* remains profoundly personal; and though every element in the play has been a theme of other poets, we know that the amalgam of these elements is Shakespeare's; we feel the presence of his single mind. The Elizabethan drama would have gone on without Shakespeare, but no one else would have written *Othello*.

There are discoveries in science like Columbus's, of something which was always there: the discovery of sex in plants, for example. There are also tidy inventions like Bell's, which combine a set of known principles: the use of a beam of electrons as a microscope, for example. Now we have to ask the question: Is there anything more? Does a scientific theory, however deep, ever reach the roundness, the expression of a whole personality that we get from *Othello*?

A fact is discovered, a theory is invented; is any theory ever deep enough for it to be truly called a creation? Most nonscientists would answer: No! Science, they would say, engages only part of the mind – the rational intellect – but creation must engage the whole mind. Science demands none of that groundswell of emotion, none of that rich bottom of personality, which fills out the work of art.

This picture by the nonscientist of how a scientist works is of course mistaken. A gifted man cannot handle bacteria or equations without taking fire from what he does and having his emotions engaged. It may happen that his emotions are immature, but then so equally are the intellects of many poets. When Ella Wheeler Wilcox died, having published poems from the age of seven, *The Times* of London wrote that she was 'the most popular poet of either sex and of any age, read by thousands who never open Shakespeare'. A scientist who is emotionally immature is like a poet who is intellectually backward: both produce work which appeals to others like them, but which is second-rate.

I am not discussing the second-rate, and neither am I discussing all that useful but commonplace work which fills most of our lives, whether we are chemists or architects. There were in my laboratory of the British National Coal Board about 200 industrial scientists – pleasant, intelligent, sprightly people who thoroughly earned their pay. It is ridiculous to ask whether they were creators who produced works that could be compared with *Othello*. They were men with the same ambitions as other university graduates, and their work was most like the work of a college department of Greek or of literature. When the Greek departments produce a Sophocles, or the literature departments produce a Shakespeare, then I shall begin to look in my laboratory for a Newton.

Literature ranges from Shakespeare to Ella Wheeler Wilcox, and science ranges from relativity to market research. A comparison must be of the best with the best. We must look for what is created in the deep scientific theories: in Copernicus and Darwin, in Thomas Young's theory of light and in William Rowan Hamilton's equations, in the pioneering concepts of Freud, of Niels Bohr and of Pavlov.

The most remarkable discovery made by scientists, I have said, is science itself. It is therefore worth considering the history of this discovery, which was not made all at once but in two periods. The first period falls in the great age of Greece, between 600 B.C. and 300 B.C. The second period begins roughly with the Renaissance, and is given impetus at several points by the rediscovery of Greek mathematics and philosophy.

When one looks at these two periods of history, it leaps to the eye that they were not specifically scientific. On the contrary: Greece between Pythagoras and Aristotle is still, in the minds of most scholars, a shining sequence of classical texts. The Renaissance is still thought of as a rebirth of art, and only specialists are uncouth enough to link it also with what is at last being called, reluctantly, the Scientific Revolution. The accepted view of Greece and of the Renaissance is that they were the great creative periods of literature and art. Now that we recognize in them also the two periods in which science was born, we must surely ask whether this conjunction is accidental. Is it a coincidence that Phidias and the Greek dramatists lived in the time of Socrates? Is it a coincidence that Galileo shared the patronage of the Venetian republic with sculptors and painters? Is it a coincidence that, when Galileo was at the height of his intellectual power, there were published in England in the span of 12 years these three works: the Authorized Version of the Bible, the First Folio of Shakespeare, and the first table of logarithms?

The sciences and the arts have flourished together. And they have been fixed together as sharply in place as in time. In some way both spring from one civilization: the civilization of the Mediterranean, which expresses itself in action. There are civilizations which have a different outlook; they express themselves in contemplation, and in them neither science nor art is practiced as such. For a civilization which expresses itself in contemplation values no creative activity. What it values is a mystic immersion in nature, the union with what already exists.

The contemplative civilization we know best is that of the Middle Ages. It has left its own monuments, from the Bayeux Tapestry to the European cathedrals; and characteristically they are anonymous. The Middle Ages did not value the cathedrals, but only the act of worship which they served. It seems to me that the works of Asia Minor and of India (if I understand them) have the same anonymous quality of contemplation, and like the cathedrals were made by craftsmen rather than by artists. For the artist as a creator is personal; he cannot drop his work and have it taken up by another without doing it violence. It may be odd to claim the same personal engagement for the scientist; yet in this the scientist stands to the technician much as the artist stands to the craftsman. It is at least remarkable that science has not flourished either in an anonymous age, such as the age of medieval crafts, or in an anonymous place, such as the craftsmanlike countries of the East.

The change from an outlook of contemplation to one of action is striking in the long transition of the Renaissance and the Scientific Revolution. The new men, even when they are churchmen, have ideals which are flatly opposed to the monastic and withdrawn ideals of the Middle Ages. Their outlook is active, whether they are artists, humanist scholars or scientists.

The new man is represented by Leonardo da Vinci, whose achievement has never, I think, been rightly understood. There is an obvious difference between Leonardo's painting and that of his elders – between, for example, an angel painted by him and one by Verrocchio. It is usual to say that Leonardo's angel is more human and more tender; and this is true, but it misses the point. Leonardo's pictures of children and of women are human and tender; yet the evidence is powerful that Leonardo liked neither children nor women. Why then did he paint them as if he were entering their lives? Not because he saw them as people, but because he saw them as expressive parts of nature. We do not understand the luminous and transparent affection with which Leonardo lingers on a head or a hand until we look at the equal affection with which he paints the grass and the flowers in the same picture.

To call Leonardo either a human or a naturalist painter does not go to the root of his mind. He is a painter to whom the detail of nature speaks aloud; for him, nature expresses herself in the detail. This is a view which other Renaissance artists had; they lavished care on perspective and on flesh tones because these seemed to them (as they had not seemed in the Bayeux Tapestry) to carry the message of nature. But Leonardo went further; he took this artist's vision into science. He understood that science as much as painting has to find the design of nature in her detail.

When Leonardo was born in 1452, science was still Aristotle's structure of cosmic theories, and the criticism of Aristotle in Paris and Padua was equally grandiose. Leonardo distrusted all large theories, and this is one reason why his experiments and machines have been forgotten. Yet he gave science what it most needed, the artist's sense that the detail of nature is significant. Until science had this sense, no one could care – or could think that it mattered – how fast two unequal masses fall, and whether the orbits of the planets are accurately circles or ellipses. By contrast, the decent hands that stitched Halley's Comet into the Bayeux Tapestry had felt in nature only for the drama.

The power which the scientific method has developed has grown from a procedure which the Greeks did not discover, for which I will retain the old-fashioned name of induction. This procedure is useless unless it is followed into the detail of nature; its discovery therefore flows from Leonardo's vision.

Francis Bacon in 1620 and Christian Huygens in 1690 set down the first intellectual bases of induction. They saw that it is not possible to reach an explanation of what happens in nature by deductive steps. Every explanation goes beyond our experience and thereby becomes a speculation. Huygens says, and philosophers have sheepishly followed him in this, that an explanation should therefore be called probable. He means that no induction is unique; there is always a set – an infinite set – of alternative hypothetical theories between which we must choose.

The man who proposes a theory makes a choice – an imaginative choice which outstrips the facts. The creative activity of science lies here, in the process of induction understood as the making of hypothetical theories. For induction imagines more than there is ground for, and creates relations which at bottom can never be verified. Every induction is a speculation and it guesses at a unity which the facts present but do not strictly imply. The most remarkable example is the periodic table of Mendeleef, and the whole theory of atomic structure which was ultimately created to explain it.

To put the matter more formally: a scientific theory cannot be constructed from the facts by any procedure which can be laid down in advance, as if for a machine. To the man who makes the theory, it may seem as inevitable as the ending of *Othello* must have seemed to Shakespeare. But the theory is inevitable only to him; it is his choice, as a mind and as a person, among the alternatives which are open to everyone.

There are scientists who deny what I have said – that we are free to choose between alternative theories. They grant that there are alternative theories, but they hold that the choice between them is made mechanically. The principle of choice, in their view, is Occam's Razor: we choose, among the theories which fit the facts we know now, that one which is simplest. On this view, Newton's laws were the simplest theory which covered the facts of gravitation as they were then known; and general relativity is not a new conception but is the simplest theory which fits the additional facts.

This would be a plausible view if it had a meaning. Alas, it turns out to be a verbal deception, for we cannot define simplicity; we cannot even say what we mean by the simpler of two inductions. The tests which have been proposed are hopelessly artificial and, for example, can compare theories only if they can be expressed in differential equations of the same kind. Simplicity itself turns out to be a principle of choice which cannot be mechanized.

Of course every innovator has thought that his way of arranging the facts is particularly simple, but this is a delusion. Copernicus's theory in his day was not simple to others, because it demanded two rotations of the earth – a daily one and a yearly one – in place of one rotation of the sun. What made his theory seem simple to Copernicus was something else: an aesthetic sense of unity. The motion of all the planets around the sun was both simple and beautiful to him, because it expressed the unity of God's design. The same thought has moved scientists ever since: that nature has a unity, and that this unity makes her laws seem beautiful in simplicity.

The scientist's demand that nature shall be lawful is a demand for unity. When he frames a new law, he links and organizes phenomena which were thought different in kind; for example, general relativity links light with gravitation. In such a law we feel that the disorder of nature has been made to reveal a pattern, and that under the colored chaos there rules a more profound unity.

  A man becomes creative, whether he is an artist or a scientist, when he finds a new unity in the variety of nature. He does so by finding a likeness between things which were not thought alike before, and this gives him a sense at the same time of richness and of understanding. The creative mind is a mind that looks for unexpected likenesses. This is not a mechanical procedure, and I believe that it engages the whole personality in science as in the arts. Certainly I cannot separate the abounding mind of Thomas Young (which all but read the Rosetta Stone) from his recovery of the wave theory of light, or the awkwardness of J.J. Thomson in experiment from his discovery of the electron. To me, William Rowan Hamilton drinking himself to death is as much part of his prodigal work as is any drunken young poet; and the childlike vision of Einstein has a poet's innocence.

  When Max Planck proposed that the radiation of heat is discontinuous, he seems to us now to have been driven by nothing but the facts of experiment. But we are deceived; the facts did not go so far as this. The facts showed that the radiation is not continuous; they did not show that the only alternative is

Planck's hail of quanta. This is an analogy which imagination and history brought into Planck's mind. So the later conflict in quantum physics between the behavior of matter as a wave and as a particle is a conflict between analogies, between poetic metaphors; and each metaphor enriches our understanding of the world without completing it.

In *Auguries of Innocence* William Blake wrote:

> A dog starv'd at his Master's gate
> Predicts the ruin of the State.

This seems to me to have the same imaginative incisiveness, the same understanding crowded into metaphor, that Planck had. And the imagery is as factual, as exact in observation, as that on which Planck built; the poetry would be meaningless if Blake used the words 'dog', 'master' and 'State' less robustly than he does. Why does Blake say dog and not cat? Why does he say master and not mistress? Because the picture he is creating depends on our factual grasp of the relation between dog and master. Blake is saying that when the master's conscience no longer urges him to respect his dog, the whole society is in decay (is, in fact, going to the dogs). This profound thought came to Blake again and again: that a morality expresses itself in what he called its Minute Particulars – that the moral detail is significant of a society. As for the emotional power of the couplet, it comes, I think, from the change of scale between the metaphor and its application: between the dog at the gate and the ruined State. This is why Blake, in writing it, seems to me to transmit the same excitement that Planck felt when he discovered, no, when he created, the quantum.

In my view, the appreciation of art or mathematics or any creative act is an act of re-creation. When the man makes *you* see the unexpected likeness, makes you feel it to be natural that this likeness exists, then you in your modest way are re-creating.

You re-live the act of creation; and that is why (in my view) appreciation is not passive. It is an activity of the same kind as the original act of creation, even though it is lower in intensity.

It is possible to regard creation as a special process which could express itself either in making things or in destroying them. I do not share this view. I say that the opposite of creation is not destruction but disorder. The opposite of the created work is simply chaos. And therefore, I do not agree that there is a personality which has the creative impulse in reverse, and which wants to destroy for this reason.

The act of creation is, I have said, the same in science as in art. It is a natural, human, living act. Yet, of course, a poem is obviously not like a theorem. How does it differ? That has nothing to do with how it is composed; the units differ because they match human experience in different ways. Take a theorem like the Pythagorean theorem; this is a theorem every child rediscovers. He always rediscovers it in the same form; his experience is intellectual and can be exactly matched. In the arts this does not happen. Many people are going to paint pictures with a human being and an animal, but nobody is going to paint *The Lady with the Stoat* again exactly as Leonardo did. Many people are going to write plays, not exactly like *Othello*, but on a similar theme. In the arts, it is not possible for the experience of one individual to match that of another, as if it were a blueprint. You do not read a work of art for this purpose; you re-create it, but you do not re-create the blueprint. You explore your own experience; you learn; you live; you expand inside. I have discussed these actions fully in my book *The Identity of Man*. Here I will summarize the discussion by saying that the difference between the arts and the sciences lies not in the process of creation, but in the nature of the match between the created work and your own act of re-creation in appreciating it.

One of the values which science has made natural to us is originality; as I said earlier, in spite of appearances science is not anonymous. The growing tradition of science has now influenced the appreciation of works of art, so that we expect both to be original in the same way. We expect artists as well as scientists to be forward-looking, to fly in the face of what is established, and to create not what is acceptable but what will become accepted. One result of this prizing of originality is that the artist now shares the unpopularity of the scientist: the large public dislikes and fears the way that both of them look at the world.

As a more important result, the way in which the artist pictures the world has come close to the scientist's. For example, in what I have said science is described as preoccupied less with facts than with relations, less with numbers than with arrangement. This new vision, the search for structure, is also marked in modern art.

I underline this common vision because I believe that history will look back on it as characteristic of our age. A hundred years ago the way to advance physics and chemistry seemed to be by making more and more exact measurements. Science then was a quantitative affair, and this 19th-century picture of the scientist preoccupied with numbers – the picture of Phileas Fogg at the beginning of Jules Verne's *Around the World in Eighty Days* – is still large in the popular mind.

But in fact the concern of science in our age is different: it is with relation, with structure and with shape. Today we hardly ask how large space is, but whether it is open or closed on itself. We say that rubber stretches because its atoms are strung out in chains, and a diamond does not because the atoms are locked in a closed pattern of rings. When we ask why bacteria absorb the sulfa drug on which they cannot grow, we are answered that the drug deceives them: its molecules have the same shape as the body chemical that the bacteria need. And the most arresting discovery of the 1950's was the elucidation of the geometrical arrangement by which the nucleic acid in a living cell makes copies of itself when the cell divides.

Ours is not the first age whose science is preoccupied with pattern and arrangement; Greek thought was occupied in the same way, so that Plutarch quotes it as Plato's opinion that God is a geometer. And just as Greek thought looked for the shape of things in art and in mathematics together, so our age looks for the shaping skeleton below the appearances in art as well as in science. To us the form is meaningful when it expresses the logical structure; and even in everyday things – in buildings, in airplanes and in women – we now think those shapes beautiful that, spare and direct, are dictated by the function and the structure. Certainly in works of art, what drives the best painters and sculptors today is the search for the underlying organization of nature. Unlike the Impressionists, modern painters are looking for the order below the surface, the skull beneath the skin. Abstract sculpture now often looks like an exercise in topology, exactly because the sculptor shares the vision of the topologist. And with this grand yet particular generalization, it is timely that I remind you that I am still a mathematician at heart, and that I throw open the gates of argument to the practitioners of other sciences and other arts.

DONALD W. MacKINNON

Creativity: a multi-faceted phenomenon

A native of Maine, DR. MacKINNON *received his undergraduate training at Bowdoin College and did graduate work at Harvard, receiving his Ph.D. in psychology there in 1933. He has taught at the University of Maine, Harvard, Radcliffe, Bryn Mawr, and since 1947, at the University of California, Berkeley.*

He has been a fellow at Harvard studying in Europe and has held summer teaching assignments at Salzburg, Austria, and the University of Hawaii.

Since its founding in 1949, Dr. MacKinnon has been director of the Institute of Personality Assessment and Research at Berkeley. The objective of this institute is the study of highly effective individuals. At the present time, the major activity of the institute centers upon a study of highly creative individuals and the nature of the creative process. This research has been supported by a grant from the Carnegie Corporation of New York.

Dr. MacKinnon is the author of many scientific articles and co-author of two books. He is presently writing a book which will report the findings of the institute's study of creativity in architects.

His service on boards and committees related to psychology, scholarship, and testing, are many and varied, and include work with the National Merit Scholarship Corporation and Educational Testing Service.

In 1962, Dr. MacKinnon was chosen by the American Psychological Association as the Walter VanDyke Bingham Memorial Lecturer. The Lecture on 'The Nature and Nurture of Creative Talent' was given in April, 1962, at Yale University.

In 1967, he received the American Psychological Associations Richardson Foundation Award for his research in creativity.

Many are the meanings of creativity. Perhaps for most it denotes the ability to bring something new into existence, while for others it is not an ability but the psychological processes by which novel and valuable products are fashioned. For still others, creativity is not the process but the product. Definitions of creativity range all the way from the notion that creativity is simple problem-solving to conceiving it as the full realization and expression of all of an individual's unique potentialities. One would be ill advised to seek to choose from among these several meanings the best single definition of creativity, since creativity properly carries all of these meanings and many more besides. Creativity is, indeed, a multi-faceted phenomenon.

What I am suggesting is that we think of creativity, not as a theoretical construct to be precisely defined, but rather as a rubric or a chapter heading under which a number of related concerns quite naturally fall. Conceived of in this way, there are at least four major aspects of creativity which deserve attention, namely, (1) the creative process, (2) the creative product, (3) the creative person, and (4) the creative situation. Each of these can be formulated as a question to which empirical research, if it has not already done so, can provide some answers: (1) What is the nature of the creative process? What are the qualities and kinds of psychological processes by which creative solutions to problems are achieved? (2) What are creative products? By what qualities can they be identified? (3) What are the distinguishing traits and characteristics of creative persons? (4) What are the specifications of the creative situation, the life circumstance, or the social, cultural, and work milieu which facilitate and encourage the appearance of creative thought and action?

The creative process

Those who have been fortunate enough to experience moments of high creativeness, as well as psychologists who have sought to understand the process whereby creative solutions to complex problems are achieved, are in remarkable agreement as to how the creative process is to be described. Both have noted certain distinguishable phases or stages in the process. Those that I would emphasize are the following: (1) a period of preparation during which one acquires the elements of experience and the cognitive skills and techniques which make it possible for one to pose a problem to himself, (2) a period of concentrated effort to solve the problem which may quickly be solved without much delay or difficulty, but which perhaps more often involves so much frustration and tension and discomfort that, out of sheer self-protection, one is led to (3) a period of withdrawal from the problem, a psychological going-out-of-the-field, a period of renunciation of the problem or recession from it, a time away from the problem that is often referred to as a period of incubation, which is followed by (4) a moment of insight that is accompanied by the exhilaration, glow, and elation of the restructuring 'a-ha' experience, and (5) a period of verification, evaluation, elaboration, and application of the insight that one has experienced.

The creative process starts always with the seeing or sensing of a problem. The roots of creativeness lie in one's becoming aware that something is wrong, or lacking, or mysterious. One of the salient traits of a truly creative person is that he sees problems where others don't, and it is this that so often makes him unpopular. He insists on pointing out problems where others wish to deny their existence. A constantly questioning attitude is not an easy one to live with, yet in its absence many problems will not be sensed and consequently creative solutions of them will not be achieved. It has been said of Einstein that a part of his genius, like that of all great creative thinkers, was his inability to understand the obvious.

Creativity, although presently much emphasized in psychological research and in the thinking of many intelligent persons, as evidenced by the theme of this conference, has been one of the most neglected topics in the history of mankind. For far too long the creative process was thought of as inherently mysterious and unanalyzable, and the creative person as too sensitive and precious to be subjected to study. Today the creative process is recognized as scientifically researchable, and the creative person as capable of being assessed as any other human being.

It is misleading to refer to the creative process as though it were a single, unitary process. The term should be thought of as no more than a convenient summary label for a complex set of cognitive and motivational processes, and emotional processes too, that are involved in perceiving, remembering, imagining, appreciating, thinking, planning, deciding, and the like. Such processes are found in all persons, not merely in a chosen few, though obviously there are wide differences in the quality of these processes as well as in the degree to which persons are creative.

There are several factors that serve to block or inhibit a person's creativeness, first among them being the failure to see a problem where one exists. He who is overly satisfied with himself or with the situation in which he finds himself will be blind to shortcomings in himself or in his surroundings. Some measure of dissatisfaction with the present state of affairs – because it isn't clear or is incomplete or is in some sense disturbing – is a prerequisite for any attempt at transformation and improvement. There is the necessity in the creative person for what the poets have called 'divine discontent' and what Voltaire chose to call 'constructive discontent'.

But becoming aware of a problem either by sensing it oneself or by having it pointed out by another will not insure that the problem will be solved creatively or even that it will be solved at all. There is the necessity that the problem be properly perceived and correctly defined. When it is, the very statement of the problem carries within it hints or suggestions as to how it may be solved. Improperly formulated, the problem may appear to be insolvable and, indeed, because of that very fact alone, it may be so. The first task, then, for one who is going to solve a problem creatively is to make a sufficient analysis of the complex situation, narrowing down and simplifying it, until the crucial difficulty in the task is isolated.

Since most problems are neither clearly perceived nor correctly defined, the first task of a creative person, after becoming aware of a problem, is to see it in a light different from that in which it is originally presented. He must, in other words, be cognitively flexible, capable of reorganizing and restructuring the problem so that possibilities of the solution are carried within the new reformulation of it, if he is ever to solve it creatively.

Another important factor that may hamper attempts to solve problems creatively is the amount and availability of information or knowledge pertinent to the solution. Obviously, too little information or unavailable information will impede or even make impossible the solution of a problem; one must have the relevant and necessary information if the problem is to be solved. It is equally true, however, that too much information can interfere with the attainment of a creative solution. An excessive input of information can produce a state of what has been called 'mental dazzle' which makes the problem look more complex than in actuality it is.

In many fields of endeavor the day has long since passed when the 'primitive' is likely to be highly creative. In our scientifically and technologically advanced society the well-trained and highly educated professional must possess a large body of expertise. But, as just noted, too much knowledge can be a dangerous thing for creativity. It is not by chance that most of the major inventions have been made by persons who have not been experts in the field of their inventions. The expert, all too often, 'knows' both on theoretical grounds and on the basis of empirical findings that certain things are not so or just cannot be done. The naive novice ventures what the expert would never attempt, and often enough succeeds. Some of the most creative scientific achievements have been accomplished by men who, trained in one field, enter upon another, there to formulate new problems and execute novel experiments with the expertise gained from earlier training and experience but at the same time with the naive perception of a stranger in a foreign land. The creative person is one who in his intellectual endeavors reconciles the opposites of expert knowledge and the childlike wonder of naive and fresh perception.

As a result of our training as well as of our experience most of us are disposed to approach any problem with as analytical an attitude as we can muster. We would be ill advised to do anything else, yet paradoxically, efficient, economical, and analytical perception is sometimes the enemy of creative insight. Analysis disassembles a whole into its parts, separating out from one another the elements of a problem. At a certain stage this is necessary, if progress is to be made; but in the course of analyzing a problem certain attributes which pertain to the phenomenon as a whole may be destroyed with the danger that eventually one 'cannot see the woods for the trees'. What is then needed, if there is to be a creative reorganization, is a compensating, free, spontaneous look at the whole situation, a naive and childlike apprehension of what is there. Such an attitude encourages the use of imagination in the form of analogies, and similies, and metaphors which are so crucial in the insightful reorganization of any problem.

There is much more to say about the creative process; other aspects of it will come to view as we turn our attention to the other facets of creativity.

The creative product

Anything that is experienced or made by man – an idea, a work of art, a scientific theory, the design of a building – may be a creative product; but if they are to qualify as true creations they must first meet certain criteria.

The first requirement of a creative product is novelty; it must be original. But novelty and originality need further specification, for one must at once ask, within what frame of reference or range of experiences is the product original – that of an individual, or of a group, or of mankind. Much that a young child experiences and many of his ideas will be new to him and in that sense creative for him, but if these experiences and ideas are had by practically all children they are not creative products for the society in which the child lives. Similarly, a man may think a thought new to him, yet it may be one of the most common thoughts in the whole world. Thus the creativeness of a product when judged in terms of novelty, originality, or statistical infrequence is always relative to a given population of products. Those that are most creative are the ones that are novel or original in the experience of an entire civilization or of all mankind.

Mere novelty of a product does not, however, justify its being called creative. There is a second requirement, namely, that the product be adaptive to reality. In other words, it must serve to solve a problem, fit the needs of a given situation, accomplish some recognizable goal. And this is as true for the expressive arts as for scientific and technological enterprises; in painting, the artist's problem is to find a more appropriate expression of his own experience; in dancing, to convey more adequately a particular mood or theme, etc.

A third requirement that a fully creative product must meet is that the insightful reorganization which underlies it be sustained, evaluated, elaborated, developed, and communicated to others – in words, the creative product must be produced.

These, as I see it, are the three absolute criteria of a creative product. There are additional and, if you will, optional criteria. The more of them that are met, the more creative the product, for, though there may be many correct solutions to a problem, not all solutions are equally good. Some are more elegant than others. Thus there is a fourth criterion, met by a truly creative product, which demands that the answer which the product yields be an aesthetically pleasing one. The solution must be both true and beautiful.

The fifth and highest criterion for a creative product is seldom met since it requires that the product create new conditions of human existence, transcending and transforming the generally accepted experience of man by introducing new principles that defy tradition and change radically man's view of the world. Products of this level of creativeness would include the heliocentric theory of Copernicus, Darwin's theory of evolution, and Freud's psychoanalysis.

A distinction is frequently made between two kinds of creativity and creative products – artistic and scientific. Artistic creativity, it is said, results in products that are clearly expressions of the creator's inner states, his needs, perceptions, emotions, motivations, and the like. In creating them he has a deeply moving emotional experience or encounter. In scientific creativity, it is argued, the product is unrelated to the creator as a person, who in his creative work acts mainly as a mediator between externally defined needs and goals, operating on some aspect of his environment so as to produce a novel and appropriate product, but he adds little of himself or of his style as a person to the resultant. Such a description of scientific creativity is, however, more appropriate to technological and inventive activity in which the affective life of the worker plays relatively little role. In the highest reaches of science as well as of art it seems clear that there is a connection, albeit a mysterious one, between affectivity and the creative process. In the arts, the great productions appear to be exquisite attempts to resolve an internal turbulence. In the sciences, the important theoretical efforts seem to be personal cosmologies as much as anything else (witness Einstein, the prime example; Sherrington, Cannon, Born, Schrödinger, and others). The validity of the creative product thus is almost (but not quite) incidental to the forces driving its expression. And the forces are largely affective.

There is another sense in which the distinction between artistic and scientific and technological is often obliterated, for surely there are domains of creative striving in which the practitioner must be both artist and scientist-technologist; architecture would be a good example. Great architectural designs are surely expressions of the architect and thus very personal products at the same time that they impersonally meet the demands of external problems. Surely, however, creative products are not limited to the realms of art and science and technological invention but include such intangibles as those educational, social, business, and political climates which permit and encourage those who are in them to develop and to express to the full, their creative potentials. In some cases even a person may be thought of as a creative product. These are the persons who have been variously called, by Goldstein, and Maslow, the self-actualizing person, by Jung, the individuated person, by Rogers, the fully functioning individual, by Fromm, the productive character, and by Rank, the artist, the man of will and deed who makes a work of art out of his own life.

The creative person and the creative situation

The other two facets of creativity, the creative person and the creative situation, I shall discuss together rather than separately, for it is to the answering of these two related questions that the researches in the Institute of Personality Assessment and Research have contributed most directly and importantly. Our present concern with creativity is the most recent expression of the continuing research objectives of the Institute, namely, the delineation of the characteristics of individuals, who, in their personal lives and professional careers, function with high effectiveness, and the discovery in the life history, in the present life circumstance, and in the structured personality, of those factors which contribute to and make possible personal and professional effectiveness.

Although our researches have revealed differences among creative workers in the several fields we have studied, our most impressive finding is the large number of attributes which they share in common. I shall therefore, and especially in view of the constraints of time, limit my remarks to a presentation of a few of the more salient characteristics of all the creative groups we have studied, emphasizing what is most generally true of creative persons.

Few would doubt that it is the events of the early years of life and the social and intellectual climate in which a child grows up that are most crucial for the nurturing of creative potential. However, again due to the constraints of time, in discussing the creative situation, I shall restrict myself to suggesting, mindful of the traits of creative persons, ways in which colleges might structure the curriculum and provide intellectual climates most likely to foster the creative potential of their students.

Creative persons are, in general, intelligent, whether their intelligence is estimated from the quality of their accomplishments or measured by standardized tests. Yet we have found essentially zero correlation between the measured intelligence of our creative subjects and the judged creativeness of their work; and, similarly, little relationship between their academic performance both in high school and in college, and their judged creativeness. One obvious implication of this finding is that a college which desires to nurture creativity should perhaps start by examining its admissions policy. If it wishes to admit mainly those who will do well academically it should, as most colleges in the past have done, give preference to those whose grades in high school are good and whose scores on tests of scholastic aptitude are high since it has been repeatedly shown that these are the best predictors of academic achievement in college. If, however, a college seeks students with creative potential, it will inquire about the creative accomplishments of its applicants during the high school years or even earlier, for these are the best predictors of creative achievement in college and thereafter.

A certain level of intelligence is required for satisfactory academic achievement in college, and we should not delude ourselves into thinking that we can lower drastically the level of intelligence required for admission and still have students capable of meeting the standards of higher education as we have known them in the past. Traditionally there has been an over-emphasis on intellect and aptitude in college admissions. The need to right that imbalance by giving more weight to factors of interest and motivation is clear; it is important, however, not to move so far as to substitute a new imbalance for the old. Non-intellective factors are no more the sole determinants of creative performance than intellective factors were in an earlier day thought to be, but they obviously need to be taken into account in selecting students.

Creative persons are independent in thought and action and it is this independence of spirit that may well account for the lack of correlation between their high school and college grade point averages and their subsequently demonstrated creativeness. Typically, they earn high grades in courses which interest and challenge them and poor grades in those that do not. Thus I would suggest that in selecting students at both the graduate and undergraduate levels more attention be paid to the pattern of grades earned rather than to mere grade point average or rank in class.

Since it is a fundamental characteristic of those with creative potential that they are strongly motivated to achieve in situations in which independence of thought and action are called for and have much less interest or drive to achieve in situations which demand conforming behavior, as much opportunity as possible should be provided for independent study and research. All too often, however, in most colleges independent study is restricted to honor students, and while they too can profit from such a program, there would seem to be little justification for excluding from such opportunities the very students likely to profit most from them.

Creative persons are open to experience both of the inner self and the outer world. As between perceiving (becoming aware of something) and judging (coming to a conclusion about something) creative persons are on the side of perception, receptive, and seeking to know as much about life as possible. Their perceptive attitude expresses itself in curiosity; it is the hallmark of their inquiring mind. Moreover, creative persons are discerning, observant in a differentiated fashion; they are alert, capable of concentrating attention and shifting it appropriately; they are fluent in scanning thoughts and producing those that serve to solve the problems they undertake; and, characteristically, they have a wide range of information at their command. From an associationistic viewpoint, creativity is putting the elements of one's experiences into new combinations, and the more bits of information one has and the more combinations that are formed, the more likely it is on purely statistical grounds that some of them will be creative.

Colleges can nurture and reward the perceptiveness and curiosity of their students by providing a wide variety of courses of study. All too often, though, they curb the far-ranging interests of their students by demanding that an excessive number of units of study be taken in the major subject. In all education and especially in professional education an openness of mind and thus the creative potential of students can be fostered by a broadening of their experience in fields of study beyond their specialty. Such wanderings should be encouraged for they provide the student with that range of information and knowledge without which the highest levels of creative achievement are unlikely to be reached.

The creative person's perceptive openness to his inner life, to his feelings and emotions, to his imagery and symbolic processes, and to much that in others remains unconscious, provides not only multiplicity and richness of experience but also the experience of conflicting opposites and at times even of chaos. But without such psychic turbulence combined with an independence of spirit one is not likely to grow creatively. We who are teachers need constantly to remind ourselves that students who combine these traits will often enough act in ways that are disturbing to us. What we need at such times is some of the tolerance that they show if we are genuinely to support and encourage them in their creative striving.

Creative persons are intuitive both in their perceptions and in their thinking. Keenly perceptive as they are, they do not remain unimaginatively focussed upon what is given by the senses. Rather, they immediately grasp the deeper meanings, the implications, and the possibilities for use or action of that which they experience.

Traditional emphases in education – rote learning, learning of facts for their own sake and unrelated to other facts, repeated drill of material, precise memorization – are often enough valuable and required, but they contribute little to the nurturance of the processes of intuition and, indeed, seem almost designed to inhibit them. If intuitive powers are to be strengthened quite different exercises are required, for example, transferring of training from one subject to another; searching for common principles in terms of which facts from quite different spheres of knowledge can be related; developing a feeling for analogies, similies, and metaphors; seeking the symbolic equivalents of experience in the widest number of sensory and imaginal modalities; engaging in imaginative play; training in retreating from the facts in order to see them in larger perspective and in relation to more aspects of the larger context thus achieved.

Creative persons prize most highly the theoretical and the aesthetic. Their valuing of the theoretical is congruent with their intuitiveness, for both orient them to seek a deeper and more meaningful reality beneath or beyond that which is present to their senses.

The theoretical value is the highest value in scientific and scholarly research. One of the best ways for a professor to nurture the theoretical interests of his students is to engage them in his own researches and not merely as laboratory assistants or technicians, but as full-fledged collaborators in all phases of the research and most importantly in its conceptualization and planning. An even better way of fostering the development of students' theoretical interests is, of course, to encourage them to formulate their own problems and to design and execute their own researches.

The truly creative person is not satisfied with the solutions to his problems unless they are also aesthetically pleasing, unless, to use the mathematicians term, they are elegant. The aesthetic viewpoint permeates all of the work of the creative person, and it should find expression in the teaching of all skills, and disciplines, and professions if creativity is to be nurtured.

The Swiss psychologist, Carl Jung, described human nature as ruled by a law of complementariness: the tendency for every trait of man's conscious and manifest personality to be matched or complemented by its opposite in his unconscious and undeveloped self. Those aspects of self and experience which are unconscious and unexpressed in man partake of these characteristics for one of three reasons: either they have been neglected because conscious attention was never paid to them, or they have been repressed or suppressed because to experience them would be too painful, or they have remained undeveloped and unexpressed because the conscious ego, the person, is not yet mature enough to experience them. To experience what is unconscious and to give expression to it in a fully conscious manner is not easy and often enough painful and frightening. Consequently, most persons live a sort of half-life, giving expression to only a very limited part of themselves, and realizing only a few of their potentialities. In contrast, the creative person has the courage to experience the opposites of his nature and to attempt some reconciliation of them in an individuated expression of himself.

The most salient mark of a creative person, the central trait at the core of his being is, as I see it, just this sort of courage. It is not physical courage of the type that might be rewarded by the Carnegie Medal or the Congressional Medal of Honor, although a creative person may have courage of this kind, too. Rather, it is personal courage, courage of the mind and spirit, psychological or spiritual courage that is the radix of a creative person: the courage to question what is generally accepted; the courage to be destructive in order that something better can be constructed; the courage to think thoughts unlike any one else's; the courage to be open to experience both from within and from without; the courage to follow one's intuition rather than logic; the courage to imagine the impossible and try to achieve it; the courage to stand aside from the collectivity and in conflict with it if necessary, the courage to become and to be oneself.

If my assessment of the creative person is correct, our task as educators, whether we be parents or professors, is not so much to teach creativity as it is to encourage our charges by ourselves being those creative persons in whom the opposites of our nature have been reconciled, creative persons with whom they can identify. Thus we each would become an educator in the original meaning of the word – one who brings forth or educes from another that which exists as a potentiality within him through being an example of that which is desired.

WILLARD F. LIBBY

Creativity in science

DR. WILLARD F. LIBBY's *1960 Nobel Prize in chemistry is one of 14 major awards he has received since 1941—the year he received the first of three Guggenheim Fellowships. The impressive list of honors includes the Columbia University Chandler Medal, Albert Einstein Medal, the American Chemical Society Willard Gibbs Medal Award, and others of equal importance.*

Dr. Libby was born in Colorado and graduated from high school in California. His college career—from bachelor to Ph.D.—began and ended (1933) on the campus of the University of California, Berkeley.

From 1933 to 1945 he was with the department of chemistry on the Berkeley campus, with the exceptions of leaves taken to Princeton, Columbia, and later for war work in the Manhattan Project.

In 1945 he became professor of chemistry at the University of Chicago's Enrico Fermi Institute for Nuclear Studies. In 1954 he was appointed by President Eisenhower to the Atomic Energy Commission and held both positions until 1959 when he resigned and returned to California and the University at Los Angeles.

He was awarded the Nobel Prize in chemistry, 1960, 'for his method to use carbon-14 for age determination in archaeology, geology, geophysics, and other branches of science.' Since 1962, in addition to his professorship in chemistry, Dr. Libby has been director of the Institute of Geophysics and Planetary Physics at UCLA.

Currently he is a director of six corporations, member of eight industrial-academic-governmental agencies, and is a consultant to such firms as the Esso Research and Engineering Company and the Rand Corporation. He is the scientific advisor for the State of Idaho.

On November, 1969, he accepted an appointment to President Nixon's Task Force on Air Pollution.

What is scientific creativity?

Scientific creativity is scientific discovery through scientific research. It is the essence of science.

Science is the study of nature by the scientific method to discover new facts and truths eventually to be formulated as natural law. The scientific method is a disciplined procedure in which objectivity is the main aim. No observation is fully accepted as scientific fact unless it is repeated and confirmed by independent observation by independent observers. The laws of statistical error are carefully used as checks on claims of accuracy with full mind of the possibility of systematic error. Training in objectivity is primary in the education of the scientist. He must be willing and ready to discard his own theories in the face of observation and, though he is not required to rejoice at such a development, he must take it as scientific progress and must try to make a new or modified theory to fit the more completely enlightened situation.

This is the method which has proven so singularly effective in attacking natural secrets. It has given mankind a cohesive and integrated approach.

I think it is fair to say that the purpose of science is creativity – therefore my paper is about science.

The discovery experience

Now let me prove that scientists are not cold fish. Let me consider the deep passion of science. I have known personally several of the greatest scientists of our time and I can tell you this: science is *not* impersonal. Every important scientist I have known has been deeply personally involved with his or her studies at every stage of the discovery experience.

The first stage – the initial idea stage – usually is one of the two most hopeful and exhilarating parts of the research experience. At this time all known to the scientist presages success and he can barely wait to prove it all out.

In the second stage he finds to his surprise that nature is different and he falls back on his training for solace and relief. The experienced scientist knows that nature yields her secrets with great reluctance and only to proper suitors. He knows also that certain supposedly inanimate objects such as scientific apparatus are animate and obey their master only if he is deserving by understanding. All this an experienced scientist knows but the poor beginner does not. The unbelievable perversities of delicate equipment unless the hands are experienced and the general irrelevance of most casual observations, these are awakenings for the young scientist – growth experiences necessary to his fulfillment.

So he struggles and tries to make his experiment work, repeats and repeats his measurements hoping to see it perform as his theory predicted. Finally and with great reluctance especially if young and inexperienced he reads nature as it really is and accepts what he has seen.

The third stage is reassurement, reconsideration, mulling over of the new data, further theorizing and finally true discovery – the realization of the true significance of what has been seen. This when it happens is the great leap forward – the real bone and muscle of scientific creativity.

Let's look at a few of the great discoveries in the physical world (as contrasted with the biological) during the last fifty years. The discoveries of the neutron, artificial radioactivity, fission, and the chain reaction. From these great experiences we may better see the nature of science and scientific creativity.

Throughout the second and third decade of this century the two great laboratories of nuclear physics – Rutherford's at Cambridge and Curie-Joliot's in Paris – steadily and thoroughly studied the effects of bombarding various materials with alpha particles. The alpha particles frequently were obtained from polonium deposited electrolytically on nickel foil in an invisibly thin layer so self absorption was negligible. The alpha particle being the nucleus of the helium atom (mass four and charge plus two, where the weight unit is 1.6×10^{-24} g and the charge unit is 4.8×10^{-10} electrostatic units) is quite heavy and travels in a straight line unless it hits the atomic nucleus. Thus Rutherford in 1912 discovered the structure of the atom by showing that deflections occurred in only one case in one hundred million atomic penetrations and then it bounced as though the entire atomic mass resided on the small center with cross section about 10^{-8} of that of the atom and therefore of density at least 10^{12} times that of ordinary matter. Well this is the background for two of the great discoveries – the neutron and artificial radio-activity.

A favorite type of study was to observe protons ejected from various metal foils such as aluminum or magnesium or beryllium when they were laid on the nickel foil plated with polonium. These transmutations had first been discovered by Lord Rutherford during World War I. For instance they would carry out

$$He_2^4 + Al_{13}^{27} = H_1^1 + Si_{14}^{30}$$

and in observing the ejected protons (H_1^1) the atomic hydrogen nuclei came out with certain discrete and definite energies; they discovered excited states in the silicon nucleus (Si_{14}^{30}). Tables of excited states were being published and budding theories of the nature and structure of nuclear matter were born. Lord Rutherford himself in the early twenties had suggested that if 92 elements with nuclear charges from $+1$ to $+92$ could exist that perhaps an element of charge zero, the neutron, might also be found.

Thus nuclear matter might consist of alpha particles, protons and electrons or of alpha particles and protons and neutrons. This idea did not catch on for some reason and thus delayed the neutron discovery for ten years for it turns out that just as protons come out of the foils so do neutrons!

The discovery was made with beryllium, for its nucleus is a particularly rich source consisting of two alphas and one neutron. Frederick Joliot and his wife Irene Curie (Madame Curie's daughter) while looking for protons from beryllium foils discovered a strange penetrating radiation coming from the foil which they ascribed to a very high energy gamma ray. Nuclei frequently emit high energy X-ray type radiation which has no particles of finite mass associated with it. Thus Si_{14}^{30} is made from Al_{13}^{27} and it is left in one or another of the excited states it will shortly thereafter emit gammas as it tumbles down from one energy level to another and finally usually within 10^{-15} sec or so reaches the lowest level, the ground state. Thus the energies of the emitted gammas correspond to the energy differences between the various proton groups. Whereas alpha particles are stopped in a few centimeters of air or a thin foil one or two thousandths of an inch thick, and beta particles (electrons emitted by atomic nuclei undergoing spontaneous radioactive emission, such as RaD [Pb_{84}^{210}], which after some thirty years on the average emits an electron and forms Bi_{83}^{210} which again emits an electron to form polonium Po_{84}^{210}, the alpha source) have ranges up to one half inch or so in paper or work or water. Gammas, on the other hand, are far more penetrating having ranges up to several feet in light material and even several inches in lead.

So the observation that an ion chamber detector would respond even with more than an inch of light material suggested gamma radiation. However, the penetrating power was so great that the energy would have to have been some 50 million electron volts (1 eV is 23,000 calories per mole or 1.6×10^{-12} ergs per atom) and since the energy of the polonium alphas was only

5 MeV, this required that Be_4^9 the atom being disintegrated would have to be unstable by some 45 MeV. The atomic masses were not known well in those days so this possibility could not be ruled out categorically but it did seem even then to be a most unlikely conclusion. But what to do? Well they published their results and suggested a strange new gamma radiation had been produced. It is hard in retrospect to see how they could have missed the neutron idea for it had been published years before. But they did and it remained for Chadwick in the Cavendish Lab at Cambridge to step in and settle the matter.

I well remember reading the Joliot – Curie paper and scratching my young head and wondering what was going on but I have the excuse that as a young student I hadn't heard of Rutherford's neutron. You see it really is difficult to make anything else out of Be_4^9 since it consists of two alphas and one neutron and the alphas are among the stablest nuclei known, i.e. to free a proton one would have to do

$$He_2^4 + Be_4^9 = H_1^1 + N_5^{12}$$

or

$$He_2^4 + Be_4^9 = H_1^1 + H_1^3 + Be_4^9$$

However, none of the nuclei N^{12}, H^3, or Be^8 are stable enough to occur naturally. To emit only a gamma ray the Be_4^9 has to be supposed to exist in a strange long lived highly excited state some 45 to 50 MeV above the ground state. In order to realize how absurd this was the total binding energy to make Be_4^9 out of four protons and five neutrons is only some 50 MeV. So the Joliot – Curie theory was hardly tenable.

A nucleus of no positive charge cannot hold electrons and as a consequence makes no collisions with the electrons in ordinary matter but only with atomic nuclei. Since nuclei are about 10^{-24} cm² in cross section the mean path length between collisions must encompass some 10^{24} nuclei per cm². So this explained the great penetrating power of the Joliot–Curie radiation. Chadwick used ordinary collision theory to calculate the momentum transfer to the target nucleus which being charged would ionize the gas in the ionization chamber to an extent proportional to this momentum transfer and by using gases of different masses showed in this way that the radiation was an uncharged particle of unit mass! Thus with air or rather N_2 gas the struck atom has mass 14 so the maximum possible momentum transfer is $2/15$ and the average is close to $1/15$. For hydrogen gas on the other hand the momentum transfer averages $1/2$ and in a head-on collision can be unity with the probability being constant for any energy interval between zero and 100 per cent. Chadwick measured the pulse size distribution in his ion chamber and found that all his observations fitted this simple, reasonable principle. Thus the neutron was born into mankind's world!

Now let's look at this episode. First we see the clinging to the established theory, the reluctance to scrap it and start over even to the extent of almost violating the most sacred of all scientific laws – the conservation of energy. Second we see that a really new idea was required – an entirely new approach. Chadwick, as you know, received the Nobel Prize in physics for this great contribution.

Two years later in 1934 the Joliot–Curie team discovered artificial radioactivity by observing that the aluminum foil was radioactive after the alpha particle bombardment which had been done so many times in studying the proton groups. The reaction involved neutron emission to form the unstable isotope of phosphorus of mass 30 which in a matter of two or three minutes forms the stable isotope of silicon of mass 30 the same one formed by proton emission. The radioactive change occurs by emission of a positive electron. The reactions are

$$He_2^4 + Al_{13}^{27} = n_0^1 + P_{15}^{30}$$
$$P_{15}^{30} = Si_{14}^{;30} + e^+$$

The positrons were sufficiently energetic to penetrate the wall of a standard Geiger counter. So the experiment itself was exceedingly simple consisting of exposing the aluminum foil to polonium alphas for a few minutes and then wrapping it around a cylindrical Geiger counter and observing its radioactive emissions and their dying off in five to ten minutes. The penetrating power could be measured by interposing absorber foils between the radioactive foil and the counter.

Thus the difficulties in this case were entirely conceptual. A theory had to be developed which lead to the test for radioactivity. Apparently the Joliot–Curies did this without publishing it. Either that or the discovery was accidental. We do not know to this day which was the case. When Joliot sent a cable announcing the discovery to Ernest Lawrence at Berkeley, Lawrence found his laboratory was radioactive from his cyclotron having bombarded many different materials with his beam of deuterons (the deuteron is the nucleus of the hydrogen isotope of mass two and consists of one proton and one neutron bound together). Within a matter of hours Lawrence found several new artificial radioactivities including radiosodium Na_{11}^{24} of 15 hours half life. In fact it seems likely that the laboratory had so much radioactivity that it constituted a health hazard!

So there is little doubt that artificial radioactivity would have been discovered accidentally very soon in Lawrence's laboratory but the fact is that it was not even suggested in the literature that such a phenomenon might be expected although immediately after the Joliot–Curie experiment was announced a theory emerged which was so simple and obvious that it is very difficult in retrospect to see why artificial radioactivity had not been looked for twenty years earlier.

The theory is that any nucleus made by transmutation and not found in nature will be radioactive and will form a stable naturally occurring nucleus and the atom containing it. Thus Al_{13}^{27} (α,n) P_{15}^{30} gives phosphorus while Al_{13}^{27} (α,p) Si_{4}^{30} does not. (The nomenclature here is alpha in and neutron or proton out.)

In a matter of a few months hundreds of new radioactivities were discovered at Berkeley. Today about one thousand are known.

Now let us analyze this case. As I see it there was no idea to lead to an experiment and the experiment came first and therefore was delayed by years beyond the time when the apparatus was available. (The polonium alpha source and the radiation detector has been available.) Thus we see the great importance of theory to science. It is just as essential as apparatus.

It seems very likely that the Joliot–Curie team had had the idea just before the experiment but certainly neither the Cavendish nor the Berkeley group had had it and we can only conclude from this experience that great ideas often are very simple and long delayed in their coming. One cannot complain if an idea as difficult as relativity theory is delayed but man's failure to predict artificial radioactivity in the fact of the great and intimate knowledge of the natural radioactivities is shattering and humbling in the extreme. We shall see another example in the discovery of atomic fission years later.

The Joliot–Curie team received the Nobel Prize in physics for their great discovery as Lawrence did also mainly for his cyclotron, however.

Our third case study is nuclear fission and its accidental discovery. Shortly after the discovery of artificial radioactivity Fermi in Rome began irradiating materials with neutrons made by Joliot's device – alphas on beryllium. He used radon gas mixed with powdered beryllium, obtaining a radon from one gram of radium in solution used normally for cancer therapy by one of the hospitals in Rome. Our own group in Berkeley followed his lead and numerous new radioactivities were discovered very quickly from (n,γ) and (n,p) reactions. Fermi's main idea was that the absence of a nuclear charge allowed the neutron to contact any nucleus even though its velocity might be essentially zero and that in fact it would react more readily at low speeds since it then would spend more time near the nucleus and thus have a better chance of reacting. The two main products were gamma rays carrying off the binding energy, usually about 8 MeV and particles such as protons and alphas. These latter usually required that the neutrons have high speed to give enough over-all energy, although this was not true in all cases. Thus by 1936 the general pattern of (n,γ) reactions to add one mass unit to an isotope of a particular element was well established. This frequently resulted in radioactivity since it often happened that the next heavier isotope does not occur in nature. Thus for ordinary sodium which has only one isotope, Na^{23}_{11}, which is stable and occurs naturally, Lawrence's radio sodium Na^{24}_{11} (20 hr average life) was readily produced by neutrons.

$$n^1_0 + Na^{23}_{11} = Na^{24**}_{11} = Na^{24}_{11} + \gamma\text{'s}$$

Fermi showed how to decelerate the neutrons as produced by the Be^9_4 (α,n) reaction to increase the reaction probability (cross section) by some hundred fold. Thus thermal neutrons which rarely could eject particles apparently were essentially reserved for the (n,γ) unit mass increase job. Thus for most of the elements it went:

$$Cu^{63}_{29}(n,\vec{\gamma})\ Cu^{*64}_{29};\ Cu^{65}_{29}(n,\vec{\gamma})\ Cu^{*66}_{29}$$

where both Cu^{64}_{29} and Cu^{66}_{29} are radioactive to emit negative beta electrons and form stable isotopes of zinc, Zn^{64}_{30} and Zn^{66}_{30}.

It was on this background that Fermi irradiated uranium with thermal neutrons from which he expected two negative beta activities for the uranium isotopes occurring naturally, U^{235}_{92} (0.71%) and U^{238}_{92} (99.29%). Although it is well to note here that his theory was wearing a little thin since no stable isotopes of the higher element neptunium (93) were known. However, he reasoned correctly that there might be sufficiently long lived and nearly stable isotopes to allow them to be produced in this way.

However he found not the two expected but dozens! This was

really a tremendous surprise and now we see a great man err. He explained this multitude of radioactivities as being transuranics in the style of $U_{92}^{238} (n,\gamma) U_{92}^{239} \to Np_{93}^{239} \to Pu_{94}^{239} \to X_{95}^{239} \to Y_{96}^{239} \to Z_{97}^{239}$ etc. and a similar chain for U^{235} – the rare uranium isotope.

It is well to recall that uranium had not been disintegrated by charge particle attack since its enormous nuclear charge (+92) required somewhat more energetic particles than Lawrence's cyclotron had been able to make, although the difference was not large and the course of history might have been changed if the requisite 10 to 15 MeV deuterons had been produced and used on uranium at Berkeley.

Well, the question of the chemical properties of the Fermi 'transuranic' radioactivities immediately arose and this was a morass, for the chemical properties of the next several elements above uranium in the Periodic Table were unknown. Irene Curie was one of the hardest workers on this problem as she published several very important papers trying to delineate the chemistry of the transuranics from the Fermi activities. Thus we see that she too apparently was going along on Fermi's partially erroneous theory. (The process he proposed does actually occur but the main part of the numerous activities were indeed products of the splitting of the atom into lighter atoms which necessarily would have the chemistry not of the transuranics but of the ordinary elements.) None of the actual researchers on the problem had had this idea, although it was suggested speculatively by the man and wife scientist team – the Noddacks. Apparently none of the radiochemists working on the puzzling problem saw this article.

Finally the great German radiochemist Otto Hahn who had helped Rutherford decipher the intricacies of the decay chains for the uranium and thorium activities took after the problem, he too following Fermi's theory but nevertheless as a matter of precaution, forcing himself to attempt to prove the Fermi activities were indeed transuranic by showing experimentally that their chemistries were different from those of the ordinary elements. Thus it was that he broke the knot by showing that one prominent Fermi radioactivity belonged to the element barium (+56) which has about half the charge and mass of uranium. He wrote in his great paper with his colleague Strassman in the December 1938 issue of the magazine *Naturwissenschaften*, 'As a physicist I do not believe this, but as a chemist I know it is so'.

Thus we see for the third time how accidental luck and a sharp eye played a large part in a great scientific discovery – probably the greatest of the twentieth century (at least until 1970).

Incidentally, Fermi was awarded the Nobel Prize, as were Hahn and Strassman as well for their work. This probably was the only time he erred seriously in interpretation of new evidence in his very distinguished career.

It is important to note the analysis of this episode that even the erroneous theory led to the revealing experiment. Since the chemistries of the transuranic elements were unknown at that time, Hahn correctly reasoned that he had to test whether the radioactivities belonged to the ordinary elements, fully expecting to find them different. So we see how theory can be useful indirectly, even when quite wrong.

Our final episode is that of the nuclear chain reactor and its discovery by Fermi and his team at Chicago on December 2, 1942. Shortly after Hahn and Strassman's announcement it was shown that the fission reaction released an enormous amount of energy, about 200 MeV, mainly as recoil energy of the two fission fragments and most importantly about three neutrons as well. I well remember the first experiment Luis Alvarez at Berkeley did was to look for these neutrons which he failed to find due to lack of adequate sensitivity apparently. The point in everyone's mind was the release of the enormous energies known to be stored in the atomic nuclei by Einstein's mass energy relation. Thus the sum of the masses of the barium and krypton atoms made by the splitting of U^{236} was less than that of U^{236} by just the correct amount $(3.2 \times 10^{-4})/C^2$ or 3.5×10^{-25} g, just the amount corresponding to 200 MeV. So it was readily calculated that the development of a chain reaction with at least one of the three neutrons always starting a second fission would cause an enormous explosion equivalent to many thousands of tons of ordinary explosive but that if the rate of fissioning could somehow be controlled, this would constitute an enormously potent new energy source.

We shall not speak here of the bomb development – the purposely uncontrolled chain reaction developed at Los Alamos but shall speak just of the peaceful controlled reaction although it was developed for a war-like use itself – the production of plutonium 239 from U^{238} by (n,γ) and two negative beta decays. Early in the post-discovery phase of fission research it was shown that it was the light and rare isotope of uranium, U^{235}_{92}, which was fissioned by thermal neutrons. Pu^{239}_{94} has the same property and even though the uncontrolled bomb chain does not allow time for thermalization, the two materials still are more readily fissioned by fast neutrons than are U^{238} or Th^{232} or any other natural material. So Fermi developed the controlled chain reactor to produce the bomb material by use of the very intense fluxes of neutrons expected in the device. However, it is essentially this reactor which is now used to generate electric power at Hanford, the site of the first plutonium reactors.

The cooling of neutrons, or their moderation as Fermi called it, is accomplished by allowing the freshly born fast neutrons (about 1 to 2 MeV) to bounce off of several lightweight atoms before again hitting uranium. Now, from what we said in the neutron discovery episode, the best moderator would be ordinary hydrogen because it has the same mass as the neutron, and on the average the energy transferred is one half. So to cool from 1 MeV to 10 eV (where the chemical bonds begin to interfere and the H atom no longer is free and thus has lost much of its moderating power) the required number of collisions is about seventeen, which should take only about 10^{-4} sec and involve migrations of perhaps one foot distance. However, the neutrons so moderated are rapidly absorbed by the H_1^1 atoms themselves to make deuterium, H_1^2, so they can't make the second fission with ordinary uranium with only 0.71 per cent U^{235} present. Modern power reactors get around this by using uranium enriched to around 1.5 to 2 per cent in U^{235} and use ordinary water both as moderator and heat transfer medium.

Fermi's problem was that he didn't have any enriched uranium nor did he have enough heavy water. Even though H_1^2 is twice as heavy as the neutron, it still is the next best moderator because it has a very low cross section for thermal neutron capture. Fermi and his distinguished colleagues Wigner and Szilard discovered and worked out these facts and conclusions and settled on graphite as the best compromise choice. This left, however, the enormous problem of producing the many tons of ultra-pure graphite (free to parts per million or less of elements with large neutron appetites such as boron and lithium and cadmium) as well as many tons of ultra-pure metallic uranium to serve as fuel. Also it was necessary to can the uranium rods in some non neutron hungry material such as aluminum to contain the fission products. With all of this in hand the final decision as to the geometrical disposition of the canned U slugs in the graphite block had to be made. All of this was done theoretically and the enormous gamble taken that the chain would propagate and do so non-explosively. This probably was the finest example of the practical application of abstruse theory to design that the world has ever seen. Fermi worked conservatively. He had a large group of scientists and engineers helping at the Metallurgical Lab at Chicago and he spared no precautions. All the neutron capture cross-sections and fission cross-sections for both fast and thermal neutrons were measured. He developed the technique of the exponential pile – a pile of graphite blocks with uranium slugs interspersed in various arrangements into which a strong beryllium neutron source activated by radium was inserted and he checked his theoretical calculations for the multiplying effect of the arrangement using neutron counters to check the flux.

He developed the control rod theory and practical design – a long rod reaching to the center of the pile of graphite which had metallic cadmium in its structure. So long as these rods were inserted in theory the chain couldn't go but when they were withdrawn and the rising crescendo of the neutron counters response told that mankind had tapped atomic energy. Two and one half years later on July 16, 1945 the first uncontrolled release occurred at Almogordo. Fermi was there too and had played an essential role there also.

I think there is no better example in all of science of a scientific research project of such enormous difficulty and importance being carried out flawlessly and without error. As I said earlier the power reactor running at Hanford today is very similar to those installed in 1943.

What do we make of this magnificent performance. Well, first you see the synthesis of the necessary experiences in the three first episodes preparing the great scientist for his extreme trial. We see the consummate calmness and faultless judgement with which he and his carefully chosen associates moved step by step relentlessly towards success. We see his willingness to subject calculations to experimental test and to subjugate theory to factual observation at every stage.

Shortly after the first Hanford reactor had begun operating for a few hours it shut itself down due to a poisoning by a fission product – an isotope of the gas xenon of larger thermal neutral capture cross-section than cadmium itself. However the Great Scientist, engineer, and his team had foreseen just such a possibility and further withdrawal of the control rods started the chain again.

We see the full power of the scientific method exhibited in this episode. Another team was working on the same problem at the same time in Nazi Germany. They did not succeed for a multitude of reasons, but that is another story.

Meaning of science for humanity as a whole

Scientific creativity – the discovery of natural law – is mankind's greatest resource for it is through scientific discovery that technological advances are made and it is technology which determines the material well-being of man in all of its aspects from his health to the length of his work week.

Note carefully the relationship between science and technology – science discovers natural law and technology applies the discoveries. Science itself is of little benefit directly except to the scientist whose joy in his work is his main spur and motivation and countries unable to make technological applications benefit little from science.

The creations of science are not engineering works or machines or products. Rather they are articles in the scientific literature openly published for the benefit of all mankind. That is science.

Application projects take many forms and generalizations can be misleading but certain general aspects can be cited. Applications usually cost much more than the science on which they are based. There are certain fields where this may appear not to be true such as high energy physics with its costly accelerators and the space program where the moon data are won at such great cost, but I plead that in both cases a decision has been made to speed the discovery process by the furnishing of enormous technological aid. Mankind could have learned about the atom by continuing the inexpensive approach of Rutherford and Joliot – Curie rather than the route Lawrence took in inventing his expensive atom smashing cyclotron. We could have continued with the more leisurely pace and it seems likely we might have come home with atomic power without the cyclotron although just barely for the discovery of the thermal fissionability of plutonium 239 was made possible by the cyclotron as was the discovery of its chemical properties so important to its separation from the irradiated slugs.

Relatively inexpensive researches on cosmic rays arriving from outer space continue to supply invaluable information to high energy physics. All in all, however, we have bought an enormous acceleration of the discovery process by these expensive aids.

Similarly in our studies of space which for centuries have been limited to astronomy and the study of meteorites hitting the earth's surface we have bought an acceleration so great as to be almost incommensurate in our space probes, terrestrial and planetary satellites, and manned flights to the moon to collect moon rocks for study. We fully expect within a year to know enough to tell us how the solar system formed. Whether this dream comes true or not, we certainly will have moved a long way toward that goal.

This week the first summing up meeting of the one hundred fifty scientists studying the material from Mare Tranquillitatus will be held and shortly thereafter the results will be published. From this great effort we hope to be able to explain the moon's properties and assess the possibility of establishing the lunar observatory for astronomical observation. Quite possibly we will get the composition of the sun as well at least in the respect of the all important helium to hydrogen ratio. The helium data are already in hand and it may be that those for hydrogen will be reported this week. The principle is that the wind of coronal material blowing outward from the sun actually hits the lunar surface and an aluminum metal foil was exposed on Apollo XI and returned for analysis.

These two examples therefore are inclined to obscure the fact that most scientific research is far less expensive than the applications to practice which are essential for human welfare. I am pressing this point because there is a widespread misunderstanding which is threatening scientific research in this country and abroad. People seem to have become obsessed by the notion that science must be what Dr. Weinberg of Oak Ridge has called Big Science. This simply is not so and if it is necessary to retrench there are ways of doing it without giving up our future. If science should be stopped by false economy, the damage to our future technological progress could be irreparable. Remember there were long dark ages before science was born and mankind must avoid reversion to that sad state.

Technology can be controlled and that is the way to save money if necessary. The trouble is that people see the immediate benefits and are less willing to forego these than they are to give up the unseen and unknown benefits of scientific creativity and kill the goose that lays the golden eggs.

Not all areas of science have been opened yet and some of these are likely to yield enormous practical benefits: human genetics and the social sciences are examples. So rather than retrenching, we should be extending the reach of the method. Physics and chemistry are well opened but biology is just unfolding. We might think a moment as to why the social sciences are so late and to far have been essentially unscientific. Chemistry throughout the dark ages was essentially in this state. It was called alchemy and consisted essentially of an unscientific collection of recipes which although useful had embodied in them no real natural law. What made a science of chemistry was the work of a few great men discovering the atoms and their abilities to form molecules. This made the difference.

It seems to me that some much fundamental break-out will have to occur in the social sciences before they can be converted into real sciences. We should strongly encourage brave, objective study of the social aspects of the human animal and learn to face facts in this area just as we have learned to do in the matter of anatomy, physiological function and the diagnosis and treatment of disease.

However, we should not settle for a name, we must insist on the reality of a strong vibrant scientific discipline devoted to the study of social behavior.

Thus in conclusion, I believe and maintain that scientific creativity in its broad sense is one of the most important factors controlling our future. No one can really afford to be opposed to real science. You can be opposed to the use planned for the knowledge, but every responsible considerate individual must favor the winning of the knowledge itself, scientific creativity.

WILLIAM ARROWSMITH

The creative university

DR. WILLIAM ARROWSMITH *has been at the University of Texas since 1958, and in his present position since 1965. He holds an A.B. and Ph.D. from Princeton (where he was a Phi Beta Kappa Scholar), a B.A. and M.A. from Oxford. He has been awarded several honorary degrees.*

His special awards and honors include Woodrow Wilson Fellowship, Rhodes Scholarship, Guggenheim Fellowship, and a recent appointment to the National Humanities Faculty.

As a visiting lecturer, Dr. Arrowsmith can list nearly 100 colleges and universities in the United States where he has been heard. In addition, he serves as a consultant to several colleges, and in the same capacity, to several business and academic organizations.

His teaching experience in his field of classics and humanities includes Princeton, Wesleyan, and the University of California, (Riverside).

Professor Arrowsmith has been responsible for the founding of three literary journals and is currently either editor or advisory editor of three publications concerned with the classics and classical criticism.

Twice he has won awards for excellence in teaching: in 1959, when he received the Bromberg Award for Excellence in Teaching at the University of Texas and in 1962, at the same institution, when he received the Morris L. Ernst Award for Excellence in Teaching. The University of Texas named him Piper Professor for 1966 'for outstanding academic achievement.'

As an author, he is responsible for a host of major publications in his field. Many of them are translations from classical languages to English. His stories, poems, reviews and articles have appeared in The Nation, New York Times Book Review, Harper's and The New Republic.

Several years ago, at a conference on the arts and the public at the University of Chicago, I urged that artists and intellectuals be invited to share – as full partners, not as occasional and barely tolerated freaks – in the task of educating a nation. Since this was an invitation which artists, mindful of their past treatment by universities, might not eagerly accept, I tried to remind them that the university was changing. 'If the university', I argued, 'as it presently exists is neither an appropriate patron nor a happy refuge, there is no reason to suppose that the university can long exist in its present form. Everything opposes its right to exist so long as it persists in imposing its 19th century forms and purposes upon an enormously different world. This is why I suggest that the artist would be wise to consider the university as something still to be shaped, as an institution which is now, because of unprecedented crisis, particularly malleable and susceptible to change. Think of the university, not as patron or refuge, but as a fatal, seminal X – an institution to be created, a chaos requiring new form, very much like the Renaissance state of Burckhardt's definition – a work of art to be made. As for the students, think of them as your future audience, the audience you do not now have; those who might be to you what Neoptolemus was to Philoctetes, or Theseus to the old Oedipus – those who end your loneliness with full knowledge of the cost and pain of having you around, because you show them what they are and who they still might be.'

It is that idea of the university as an X to be shaped, as a chaos that requires form, that concerns me here. Everybody knows that the university desperately need the talents and energies of creative men, of artists and intellectuals. But there is also a problem of context. How can the university make use of, energize, creative talents, either in its teachers or its students, unless it finds some means of becoming creative itself? The spectacle of the modern university is the dismal one, I fear, of energies that are both useful and generous being disastrously wasted, and the consequent corrosion and sickening of once generous motive – the cynicism and withdrawal and violence of the best part of a generation – is a profoundly distressing and dangerous thing. Worst of all perhaps is the failure of responsibility in those who alone have the power to act. I mean the men of knowledge: intellectuals, scientists, call them what you will. Unless the intellect can act, unless the intellectual powers available in the universities and colleges, can be brought to bear upon our problems, those problems will destroy us. Thus, if the university is to be creative, it must be creative in very radical ways indeed. It is nonsense to suppose that curricular reform and modest departmental arrangements, or the introduction to the campus of a few artists, or Nobel scientists, will do. It is the very *mission* of the university which must be changed, if the university is to become an agent of our survival and an architect of the future. And it is only by undertaking such tasks that it will be able to educate at all. The legitimacy of its authority will stand or fall as it uses, or fails to use, the power it possesses.

I begin where I must, with the humanities, not only because I know them best, but because creativity is so dreadfully and revealingly absent from them. I do not regard this as a seriously debatable point, so I will be extremely cursory. It is not polemic or analysis that is needed, but constructive proposals. But the proposals require, however cursorily, a context, a background of urgency against which they can be set.

I am not very sanguine about the survival of the official, formal study of the humanities as they exist now in American universities. They will persist, of course: imposing academic husks, respected and even revered. And there will still, I hope, be a place for their nobler scholars. But the real spirit of the humanities will vanish elsewhere, into the arts and the professions and perhaps the sciences, to reappear later as an ethos or attitude rather than a subject-matter.

The loss of the *official* humanities does not, I think, really much matter. In any case, the loss is temporary; the texts and curriculum go underground, to reappear in new ways, to be read with new urgencies. The texts are not in danger, but their *meaning* is, simply because we no longer know how to engage them, to use them. I am *not* suggesting that the times are so necessitous and urgent that we must abandon the past; we cannot do so without destroying a great and crucial part of ourselves. It is a new relation, a fresh perspective, that we need, and for that we need to suspend the old relation because it is, as so many of our students tell us, *irrelevant*. What matters is that the new humanistic spirit, that emergent *ethos*, should find a context in which to grow. The greatest obstacle is still the complacency and vanity and stupidity of the established humanities: moribund but as monstrously *there* as a dying whale. Disestablishment is what they deserve ('After such knowledge, what forgiveness?'), and disestablishment, I am convinced, is their certain fate.

Humanists have not suffered the last of their humiliations. The groundswell of public anger at a system that condones neglect of students in the name of mostly worthless research is still building. It will end by compelling drastic revision of university priorities. Neither conscience nor economy can tolerate a system that, in order to produce a tiny elite of professional scholars, stultifies thousands of potential teachers and perhaps millions of students. In the public universities there will be sharp pressure for tearing down some of the tackier (and, alas more adventurous) graduate superstructures, especially in the humanities. Not that the humanists are more guilty of triviality than their colleagues; but they are poorer and therefore more vulnerable. It is just possible that poverty *may* bring the humanists to their senses; to a valid sense of the crucial difference between curriculum and culture. I have heard professors of English heatedly argue that Melville and even Faulkner could not be properly read without their mediation. Monstrous! What is still actively alive in the culture is deadened or destroyed by being curricularized before its time. Common ground enclosed by a critic is lost ground. Losses surround us everywhere we look. (After ten years of being worked up and kneaded into courses, Black Studies will be as lost to pride and relevance as the Renaissance is useless to Italians.) A few years of genteel poverty might encourage concentration on essentials, but one wonders why poverty should work where the threat of extinction has failed.

How, then, are the humanities to be revalued? Not, I am convinced, through existing disciplines, rigid and encapsulated, where old routines and vested interests make fresh, creative response nearly impossible. Rather from outside, from the world of the professions, from the sciences, from all those critical encounters between inadequate or irrelevant ethical and wholly new situations, in which the necessity to choose is inescapable and the consequences of choice are imposing and unpredictable. Here we are always in danger of having to improvise our values as we go along, with the terrible burden of knowing that our improvisation may be fatal to others. It is a situation of tragic intensity and importance, our own reenactment of the myth of Prometheus. The cost of knowledge is necessarily imposed on the conscientious knower; only he can suffer for his gift. This is a heroic fate, and it requires both great courage and obdurate humanity. It can be refused only by deadening one's sensibility and pretending that one is not responsible, that the scientist's duty begins and ends with objectivity and detachment.

The *scientist's* duty – have I made myself clear? But it is not the scientist alone who is involved in this 'narrow place of necessity'.

The lawer, if conscientious, faces the obsolescence of his statutes, of the very principles of law perhaps; the doctor, the biologist, is trapped in an agony of choice for which his professional code provides only irrelevant answers. But these situations are the very matrix of value; from such encounters we discover who we are, what we want, what we value and love; in them we reveal ourselves. Agamemnon at the door of the palace, hesitating before trampling his heritage underfoot; poor, old mad Lear, naked in the storm; Heracles, refusing to believe in the evil of the gods who destroy him. From these encounters may be born – or reborn – a sense of conscience, or caring, of compassion, of love. Reduced to extremities, his props removed, stripped to nakedness, a man sees others in himself, himself in others; what the Greek tragedians call *aidōs*, or *sophrosynē*.

But care and compassion are a sentiment, a passion, not an ethic or a code. So this sense of care returns to the university – where professionals are trained – in quest of intellectual company, solutions, validations, rationalization, help. Help is not to be expected from academic humanists for obvious reasons; nor is it forthcoming. It comes, if at all, from the professions and other professionals. In this way the profession takes on, reluctantly and slowly, the burden of reforming itself, or of somehow adjusting of these new problematics. Out of the problems, and the professionals' necessitous involvement in them, emerges the creative response, the reforming, innovative purpose. And the consequence, profession by profession, is a slow, groping, uncertain progress toward a redefinition of the profession and its duties toward other men – toward a new humanistic ethos, an attitude toward the use of professional skill arrived at by hunch and instinct and maturing meditation. In this community of amateurs – for we are speaking of an improvised and uncertain ethos – lies, I am convinced, the future of the humanities. It is also an example of how the university can become, as an institution, creative.

I think this is a fair, if somewhat schematic, account of how change is actually occurring in the university. The primary impulse toward creative change occurs first in the professions and the sciences which are closest to the world and therefore the most sensitive to social change. The colleges of arts and sciences are full of the *chatter* of change–proposals for 'streamlining' or 'souping up' the curriculum (one notes the jazzy electronic jargon which covers the legerdemain), schemes for tandem teaching, multi-media shows and other gimmicks designed to make the ancient corpse twitch and quicken. Full of the chatter of change, but basically unchanged in attitude and perspective. In the meantime, the professions – even the colleges of engineering – are changing very gradually but also profoundly.

The incipient amateur community I am describing is of course much larger than the immediate professional community. It includes all those (e.g. many students) who feel, however incoherently, that the crucial task of the times is to create a new breed of professional as well as new institutional forms (above all, a new university) – to cope with the vast problems and value imposed by the sheer weight of numbers, by the new mass society. The formal humanism of the old university failed because it could not connect its theory with its practice; because it pretended to be only discipline and subject-matter, it lost its power as *ethos*. Behind all demands for a new university is the notion of the humanities as an attitude everywhere informing an *engaged* intellect; the very engagement, it is hoped, will sharpen and define the emergent mission. Where those demands have not been merely demands for direct political action, their effect is to make of the university a secular church. They are spiritual demands and should be recognized as such.

An example. Several months ago the Chairman of the Board of Regents of my university authorized the chopping down of a dozen magnificent liveoaks in order to make room for a culvert. Resisted by droves of student Druids perched in the doomed trees, the Chairman himself, for all the world like a modern Xerxes, cheered on the bulldozers with idiot glee. But he miscalculated: his opposition was not merely outraged students, but a sudden, large, angry, unlikely coalition of townspeople, faculty and students. He failed to observe a critical fact: ecology is not a fad, but an extremely potent focus of feeling, a force that will soon not only elect senators, but will charter universities and even churches. And the reason is that unmistakable religious and humanistic feelings find in ecology something like respectable 'scientific' status. Beneath all the talk of ecosystems lies an intimation of natural law, a feeling of religious kinship with the life of earth, and a reverence for the cosmos. So too in student revolt, one senses the prevalence and persistence of religious feelings that have, as yet no institutional home or focus.

The demand for a new, reformed university is potent precisely because the intent behind the demands is to make the university the destined home of those orphaned religious feelings. The sudden felt antagonism between state and university conceals, I suspect, the ancient quarrel between secular and spiritual institutions. Certainly the universities are being asked to assume tasks that once belonged to family and church, but for which those institutions lack the intellect – and perhaps the moral spirit – to perform. And this suggests that one of the major problems for the humanities in our time may be to recognize and redefine, in study and conduct, the religious ground of our motives and meaning. I speak, I should say, as a secular intellectual. These are not for me easy or comforting conclusions. But I am driven to them by events and trends I cannot otherwise explain.

We cannot yet say whether the effort to create a new university – that is, to create the sort of structure in which the new humanism could be defined and enlarged – will succeed. The obstacles are enormous. But so are the stakes. It would be a disaster if, in the struggle over the university, either the radicals or the scholarly conservatives won a clear-cut victory. If the university is politicized according to radical doctrine, it will forfeit its potential as a spiritual institution and become merely another, albeit intellectual, political pressure-group. The perpetuation of the old humanities by a complacent Establishment would fatally discredit the humanities (and the university) for a generation. I venture to predict that we shall, here and there, create a few institutions of a new kind – I should call them 'universities of the public interest'. They would deliberately seek to recruit and give creative direction to all those activist energies which are stifled in the existing universities. And they will be task-oriented, problem-solving universities, committed to the idea that, in a system of universal higher education, the university has a mandate which cannot be carried out except by deliberately *acting* in defence of its charter to educate *all*. That will mean taking the struggle beyond the classroom and into the street; a policy of deliberate warfare with the commercial culture. It might mean creating national newspapers or learning corporations. Or the *deliberate* effort to establish the university as a critical and corrective force in the affairs of the nation.

'The nation', said a recent editorial in *Science*, 'must consciously develop the capability to challenge government actions from a base independent of the government and its policies....' The effort to create Socratic institutions for a mass society will not be easy; it will require great political vision – but also great realism. For better or for worse, the university is *the* locus of intellectual power in a 'knowledge society'. We have no future worth thinking about unless that intellectual power is wielded conscientiously and wisely; and our only chance of doing so is to moralize university intellectuals by making them responsible for the *excercise* of the power they actually possess. Our destiny lies with the intellect. Continued impotence or irresponsibility in the intellectual means that we cannot, as a society, control our own destinies.

I am proposing, then, that we deliberately set about creating a wholly new kind of college and university – a college or university of the public interest. Its mission would be the aggressive defense of those public interests – in education, in health, in the ecology, in social justice and elsewhere – that are now threatened by syndicated greed, organized miseducation, and general vacuum of value and vision. It would refuse to be bounded by the class-room or by any limits of age or condition, and its instruments would be no less modern or powerful than those of its commercial antagonists. It would defend the social and economic and cultural interests of those minorities too weak or disadvantaged or vulnerable to defend themselves. It would attempt to make *creative* use of precisely those talents and energies whose frustration by the traditional university threaten to corrupt the better part of a whole generation and to destroy the university too. It would seek, if possible, a public charter or license and public funds as well, and the massive grounds of its request would be the stunning failure of laws, of government, of politicians, or regulatory agencies to protect the public interest. Our regulatory agencies, as we know, are almost all the creatures of the industries they were designed regulate. Against competing lobbies, the public interest is nearly helpless, wholly dependent upon a handful of superb Quixotes, like Ralph Nader, or lobbies of splendid but part-time enthusiasts and cranks, eager but mostly powerless, to protect our ears and consciences and sanity against the supersonic transport, or the Pentagon, or the media. Unselfishness is unincorporated, it has no coherent party or program, no normalized place in American life; where once family and church and school spoke for the public interest, there is now only a silence, broken now and then by the voices of angry students, gurus, madmen, and enthusiasts. In the circumstances, we must somehow normalize in our society a spiritual and anti-commercial force, a countervailing institution – a new tribunate, not of the plebs, which has its voices and power, but of the unrepresented *res publica* itself. We must somehow syndicate Ralph Nader.

Can this conceivably be done? I am convinced it can. A base, after all, exists in those institutions – the poorer liberal arts colleges, the church-related schools – which have lost their old function and have not found another. And the pluralism of these institutions – their various religious and social commitments – will make possible a happy pluralism of mission in the new universities into which they might be combined. For I assume that the public interest is too complex a matter to be entrusted to any single definition of it; it will best be served, not by some general orthodoxy of benevolence, but by competing missions and definitions. Moreover, the tasks to be undertaken are too various; we need above all the flexibility that comes of varying powers and resources. But at the start we must have one or two wholly new institutions – several universities of the public interest free to recruit wholly new faculties adapted to their ends, and to create the sort of internal structures required to carry out their missions. I do not see why federal support of these institutions could not be requested and secured. Again and again the government has sought to use the traditional university as a means of coping with social problems beyond the power of the government to cope with; and again and again the structure and staff of the university has proven intractable or intolerably clumsy to accomplish these jobs. I see no reason why government support should not be secured and a corresponding public charter created for the new university – a charter to apply knowledge to those problems on which the survival of the culture and nation depend. Once secured, such a charter could be – and certainly would be – significantly expanded.

There is also the factor of established institutional interest. We will not, I take it, persuade Harvard or Yale or Johns Hopkins to become universities of the public interest. They will remain what they now are – research universities operating in the national interest, which is only seldom the public interest. Their staff, their structure, their resources and traditions oppose their conversion to a different purpose. And this is as it should be. We need institutions as different as the men we propose to educate. And the patient, laborious reflections of the scholar and the pure scientist have as strong a claim to fulfillment as those of the applied critical intelligence of the activist. The monastic college, the public interest university, the research institute – we need them all. It would be as great a pity if the student revolt destroyed the great scholarly universities, as it would be if research were allowed to go on usurping, as it has, the place of all education in our society. By founding a new university of the public interest, we might make creative room for the frustrated energies of the student revolt, both freeing the traditional universities from the pressures that otherwise may destroy them and enabling activist students to put their energies to creative use.

The educational advantages of a genuinely pluralistic higher education would be, I am convinced, impressive. For obvious reasons a university of the public interest would not be primarily concerned with certifying its students for other professions or jobs. And by abolishing certification from the outset, we might make possible the real freedom without which real education is a mockery and real motivation crippled. Grades, I assume, would wither with degrees, since the purpose of the institution would be to complete its task and solve its chosen problems, not to rank its students for jobs or graduate schools. The student would, moreover, become a genuine apprentice and partner, learning while doing. And it is conceivable surely that the perverse aspects of the disciplinary organizations (the departments) could be severely reduced without causing real damage to the disciplines themselves. For clearly one cannot ask an institution to perform tasks or solve problems which *require* the pooling of skills and the removal of disciplinary boundaries without radically altering the existing patterns of specialization. In the present university, one can only *request* specialists to become interdisciplinary in their approaches, but there is very little likelihood of success so long as the political structure of the university rewards and perpetuates specialized research. That is, truly interdisciplinary research and teaching depend almost entirely upon the existence of general institutional goals which *necessitate* pooling of skills and approaches. It is the very nature of most of our problems that they can be solved only be men whose learning or consciences transcend the customary goals of the disciplines. And this crucial pooling of skills also suggests a way of restoring what is now so lacking in institutions of higher learning – a sense of community founded upon common concerns and upon an end larger than 'the pursuit of truth'.

Clearly institutional resources and traditions should be closely adapted to the tasks chosen. They should also be limited to those tasks that could be meaningfully completed by colleges and universities. It would be folly for institutions to commit themselves, either singly or together, to tasks they cannot conceivably complete or that might better be carried out by other social institutions. The approach in general should be gradualistic and provisional – an attempt to define in action how cultural changes can best be carried out by institutions that must prove their own competence at problem-solving before earning general public acceptance and a right to a larger role. Spiritual institutions are neither made nor remade overnight; one must first create a flexible and efficient structure, recruit the right sort of faculty and students, create the appropriate ethos, etc.

A few examples.

First, educational technology. Large corporate interest are now invading the field of computerized instruction, and there is very little evidence that the purposes of these large industries are supportive of, or even congenial to, the educational role of universities. The risk is high that programming will be done according to quite unsophisticated eductional assumptions, simply because these are the most easily programmable. One can, after all, program modern language instruction according to Berlitz methods or one can create more sophisticated programs according to more humanistic and literary assumptions. We can be virtually certain that the crudest sort of quantification will be the rule in programmed instruction in the social sciences – to the detriment of the social sciences. What is needed is the threat of quality and educational sophistication in the marketplace – where no such threat currently exists. Unless universities act in defense of their own educational assumptions, their control of their own policies and curriculum will be jeopardized. And they have a responsibility to act in accordance with their new mission to educate universally. The reason they have not acted is their own passive epistemology and their own cumbersome structures. They are also, it seems, reluctant to embark upon modern techniques of diffusion – which require the creation of quite complicated and unfamiliar techniques and organizations. Yet just as they once created presses and publishing houses to diffuse the knowledge they created, so they are now obligated to take the risks involved in computerized instruction. Those risks may be intolerably high, and I am not suggesting that universities should climb on the bandwagon of educational technology, but rather that they should involve themselves in it in order to protect their own educational interests.

Clearly no attempt to create a 'learning corporation' could be undertaken without quite massive technological and academic resources. A consortium including at least one or two major technological universities would be necessary, and there would also have to be public funds available to support the high risk of failure. Yet the public interest is clearly involved – if the public interest includes educational as well as information (or syndicated and computerized misinformation). And the universities cannot ignore their responsibility to promote the general enlightenment.

A second example. Several years ago Harry Ashmore of the Center for the Study of Democratic Institutions remarked:[1] 'The university performs some of the teaching function and some of the producing function for the arts but everybody seems to agree that the traditional function of the university and the traditional function of the arts have not been melded so far. Yet the university... should have a great critical role in all the areas of society, particularly culture... I went the rounds of colleges for several years – armed with some money too – trying to find a university that would establish... a critical commission on the mass media; which among other things would render a verdict, at least annually, on how the mass media were performing. I got the same answers from all of them: the idea was unconventional or controversial, it wasn't something the universities ought necessarily to be doing... Despite these universal negatives, I still think this country and its mass media need some independent center of criticism, and I still don't see why it shouldn't be lodged in a university.'

In this proposal, I am convinced, lies one of the major tasks of the new university or college. At present there is no responsible agent in the culture for the systematic critical review and assessment of the major mass-institutions of the culture. The mass media are almost wholly exempt from serious or sustained criticism, and this exemption is, given the influence of the media on our lives, both intolerable and disastrous. For better or worse, our lives are shaped by what we see and hear, by the information made available to us, by the level of public discussion as that level is mirrored in the media, by the kind of intelligence brought to bear on our common problems. And the criticism of the media is surely a task compatible with the function of colleges and universities – their charter, as educators of almost every-

---

[1] *The Arts in a Democratic Society*. Center for the Study of Democratic Institutions, Santa Barbara, California, 1966, page 22.

body, to protect the general enlightenment. If the university's old teaching function has been diminished, the reason is not merely the prestige of research, but the general recognition, especially among students, that the kind of teaching the universities are traditionally committed to has, even when good, become increasingly marginal, and impotent. Impotent above all because it has permitted its natural partner, the new media, to become its actual antagonist; and because it has not dared to enter the lists against this new antagonist. If the university is to teach, to use its educational influence, it must be willing to take its ideas into the marketplace, to compete Socratically, with the commercial sophists and the corrupters of the youth.

Ashmore's project should prove congenial to universities and/or colleges. For one thing, it suggests how, without radically altering existing structures, the university might field its own sense of the past, or of complex ideas, or of desirable and valuable cultural goals, in such a way that students might actually see for the first time the relevance of knowledge, the relevance of ideas. For another, it suggests how some of our hopelessly paralyzed disciplines might regain vigor. *Suppose*, for instance, that our university practice suggested that a knowledge of Euripides might be useful for something besides reading Racine – might, that is, be useful for criticising Bergman, or the media shows, or the underground art film. *Suppose* that we actually licensed in our practice the old humanistic idea that a mind trained on the greatest art of the past is, of all minds, the one best equipped to move in the present, to detect the fraud from the true, etc. Suppose we insisted, in short, that the present actually was what Whitehead called it – 'holy ground' – and that all our knowledge of the past was intended to make the present holier still...

Again, the notion of a good national newspaper is admittedly remote and unlikely. At present the country possesses only one nationally distributed newspaper (*The Wall Street Journal*, published simultaneously in at least a dozen cities) and only three of requisite quality and standards (*The New York Times, The Washington Post* and the *Los Angeles Times*). But technologically there is no reason why we should not have a national newspaper, nor is there any reason why that paper should not, or could not, be produced by a consortium of regionally distributed universities. Clearly most state universities are too politically sensitive to play a major editorial role in such a venture, but it should not be beyond the powers of a consortium of large private universities. with help from liberal arts colleges and church-related schools, such an effort would obviously require a large-scale application of institutional resources, and major institutional restructuring. But since at least one of our purposes is precisely to effect national restructuring of universities in terms of a new university mission, such restructuring is indispensable. One can imagine for instance, that the old structures would simply wither and that new tasks-defined structures would arise – at least in that part of the institution responsible for the job. Journalism schools, however, might be wholly recreated and reinvigorated, since their task would be to create responsible and educated journalists for a new kind of journalism. Obviously no major national newspaper could conceivably be produced by the schools of journalism as they now exist; on the other hand, once we create a job-market for good journalists, it will no longer be necessary, as it now is, to produce pre-corrupted journalists for a corrupt national and local press. To put it another way: the university must deliberately create anew those institutions – such as new colleges, newspapers, etc. – for which it now trains personnel. Indeed, a major part of the troubles of the university come directly from the corruption of the institutions whose personnel the universities now train. The general corruption of the American press and the wretched standards of newspaper journalism are not, I fear, something the university can reasonably be held responsible for; yet the university cannot realistically train personnel for such a press unless it either consents to the general corruption by accepting it or strives to create a genuine alternative – which means a different kind of newspaper, a press which a man need not sell his soul in order to work for. Etc., etc.

It will doubtless be objected that such tasks as these are not the responsibilities of the university, and that universities will fail if we impose on them the immense burden of redeeming a commercial culture against its wishes. Wouldn't it be saner for the university to perform its limited role as a center of intellect and to leave moral and social tasks to the church, the family, and government? Clearly, there would be no *need* to ask the university to assume responsibilities that belong, say, to the churches and the family, if there were the slightest chance that these institutions could cope with the problems. But there is none. Family and church are, if anything, in even worse shape than the university – and for much the same reasons. Hence, they have neither self-confidence nor intellectual skills necessary to cope with the crucial and distinctive fact – the *intellectualization* of our problems. The university, on the other hand, possesses intellectual skill but has disowned its moral responsibility by refusing to apply its knowledge. And, since there is no prospect whatever of endowing either church or family with the necessary intellectual power, I see no alternative except to moralize the university, to make of it – let me say it – a secular church. Admittedly, the prospect is unlikely in the immediate future, but there are, I think, very real forces for change.

For one thing, it is not in the self-interest of a majority of the country's colleges and universities to go on consenting to their own mediocrity. And this is all that most can expect, given their resources, and the hideously competitive struggle for professional distinction among the leading universities. Hence there is at least a chance that those institutions which can expect no prizes in the professional race – the church colleges, the poorer and more isolated liberal arts colleges, the community colleges – will abandon that struggle in order to create a different game.

What they may do is, I think, already tolerably clear. It can be seen in the decisive trend toward activism and service among students and faculty; in the emerging social programs of many of the church colleges; in the desperation of the cities and a dawning recognition of the potential of higher education for cultural renewal. Here, for instance, is former Commissioner of Education Harold Howe, III:

> The world of today demands that our colleges and universities be more than centers of learning and enlightenment. They must be more than research centers where ghetto pathologists analyze the underlying causes of riot.... They must turn all their resources and faculties to the problems of the survival of the communities of mankind....

And this call is immediately picked up by Samuel Gould of the State University of New York:

> Human culture is faced with the greatest peril of its history.... The university can and must devise new ways of contending with it... It is the only instrument I know of that can do this job.

One may legitimately doubt whether universities possess the moral skill and humanity to do the job properly, but those virtues can only be acquired by accepting the moral responsibility.

Moreover, colleges and universities stand to gain enormously by accepting such responsibility. Take community, for instance. Universities are commonly called 'communities of scholars', but anyone familiar with them knows that this is now merely nostalgic rhetoric. The only real community on most university campuses today is the disciplinary guild; it is the guilds, not the size, which have killed the larger intellectual community But community is surely not impossible, provided there is a context in which professionals, committed to common or related tasks, can *pool* their skills in fresh ways for significant tasks. Such tasks – and such incipient community among faculties – might eventually bring the students, now so estranged from the university, back into the community too.

The academic disciplines would also benefit, if the university were truly committed to applying its knowledge and skills. For application of intellect would tend to reconnect theory and practice, thought and action now so terribly divorced in actual instruction, above all at the graduate level. We have not yet begun to realize, I think, the damage that has been done to our students and studies alike by the dreadful snobbery of theory to which we are now so prone. Whitehead wrote:

> I lay it down as an educational axiom, that in teaching you will come to grief as soon as you forget that your pupils have bodies... Firsthand knowledge is the ultimate basis of intellectual life... To a large extent book-learning conveys second-hand information and as such can never rise to the importance of immediate practice. *Our goal is to see the immediate event of our lives as instances of our general ideas* (italics mine). What the learned world tends to offer is one second-hand scrap of information illustrating ideas derived from another second-hand scrap of information. The second-handedness of the learned world is the secret of its mediocrity. It is tame because it has never been scared by facts.

It is my conviction that we should deliberately set about scaring the learned world with facts. (The terrible wrong is that men should know so much and lack the sense to be scared.) The simplest way of doing so is to contrive a context in which learning would be confronted with the responsibility for the world that learning has created. Let us valorize learning by demanding that the creators of knowledge be held accountable for its application. How else can moral skills be created? Since intellect is power, intellect no less than power must be held accountable, This, I think, is the only way, short of chaos or cataclysm, by which human life and the human enterprise can be resolved. Charge learned men, charge the schools and universities with the

---

[1] *The Aim of Education*, New York 1957, pages 78–79.

responsibility for safeguarding what is worth keeping in the old tradition, or for the creation and diffusion, by example and instruction, of new values. Better yet, let the universities, or some of them claim this as their role. If the life of the mind and the spirit, if the common interest, are properly their business, let them prosecute that business with all the energy and intelligence at their disposal. Why should they meekly accept restriction at the hands of every selfish force in modern society? Why should they accept educational suicide? If they can be persuaded to accept the responsibilities implied by their traditional mission and their new power, they cannot refuse to act. And such action is the only thing that might create the values that we honor but fail to practice. The consequence would be a kind of culture, a valid general education. General education, I suggest, is not a curriculum, but a project for a curriculum that has yet to be created or recreated. The folly lies in thinking that curriculum can be created simply by the study that we have not ourselves reenacted. Until Prometheus suffers for his knowledge, until he puts it to responsible human use, he is irrelevant as any specialist. But there is even less to be said for the man who neither steals fire nor suffers, but merely expounds on the story. Certainly he is less educational than he might be, if he took the risk of the tale he taught.

 I repeat: the universities are deeply implicated in the disorder they so rightly deplore. If the radical knowledge they helped to create has rendered the old culture and its institutions obsolete, they cannot disown their responsibility for that knowledge or its humane application. The colleges and universities must become makers of the new culture and custodians of the culture generally. Their power to educate will eventually derive from their effort to create the culture apposite to our possibilities and our problems. Success is perhaps hardly to be hoped for, but for education the effort is what counts. For the effort implies the freedom to shape one's self and one's world. A liberal education founded upon the spectacle of powerlessness and the conviction of impotence ceases to be liberal; if care and compassion for men are absent, it also ceases to be humane. Students these days are increasingly inclined to ascribe our paralyzed culture to the operation of what they call 'The System' – a malignant Establishment Thrush that everywhere blocks the efforts and aspirations of good men. But those who, like myself, find this theory of history silly, seldom note that it is merely a romantic reflection of the prevelant fear of freedom, and the academic faith in principled impotence.

It is the almost instinctive rejection of the prevalent impotence, the academic failure of nerve, that has led the young – whose lives, as Aristotle said,[1] are regulated more by moral feeling than by reasoning – to demand that institutions declare their 'relevance' in practical and concrete ways. By so doing they impute to the university a moral authority it altogether lacks. But the ascription is revealing; the expectation is proper. What impresses me in many students is the passionate desire to shape events, to give the lie to the 'System', to create, by the vigor and vividness of their own deliberate action, a new moral order. These efforts have often been disfigured by violence, stupidity, and demagoguery; but the fact of affirmation and moral seriousness are indisputably there. And that fact is a standing reproach to the practice of universities, their inability to enlist, or put to any serious social or cultural purpose, so much high-minded, or merely mindless, energy. Where they should provide models, they offer obstacles which turn out, on closer inspection, to be rationalizations of selfish professional behavior. The function of the university is not to repress or paralyze those energies, but to suggest how they might find meaningful fulfillment and creative direction. John Gardner writes:

---

[1] *Rhetoric*, II.

> One of the most difficult problems we face is to make it possible for young people to participate in great tasks of their time... instead of giving young people the impression that their task is to stand a dreary watch over the ancient values, we should be telling them the grim but bracing truth that it is their task to recreate those values continuously in their own behavior.[1]

This ironically, is what the young are now saying to us, insisting, clamorously and incoherently, that the university should enfranchise and corroborate, through action and moral involvement, their conviction that human courage and compassion and initiative matter.

Finally, imagine the university consciously operating within a framework of dynamic change, a university founded on mutability of the modern physical universe. This is where the university belongs: at the frontiers. We can no longer afford institutions of higher learning, whose real model is a vanished universe. Nor can we afford universities which are themselves servants of an America which has become, in somebody's happy phrase, 'a middle-class *ancien regime*'. In a world of difficult change, the university must be the radical minister of change.

It is because I have faith, probably irrational, in the power of intellect – and in the university as a bastion of intellect – to renew itself, that I set such emphasis upon the creative role of the university in the moral renewal of the culture. In modern times almost the whole job of culture has been dumped upon the universities, and it is hardly surprising that they should blunder and falter under the burden. But make no mistake about the burden. Because of the torpor and indecisiveness of the churches, the erosion of communities and family life, the only potentially significant moral and cultural force remaining is the universities and colleges. Already the universities have absorbed most of the country's major artists; of every conceivable expertise except moral courage and practical organizational intelligence, they are

---

[1] *Self-Renewal*, pages 125–26

the capitals. But ultimately they draw their power from their educational role, and this means that they must be able to command the moral respect, and to enlist the moral energies, of those they are presumably educating. They cannot *educate* on any other terms.

If a student is serious, he rightly asks of his education that it give him some sense of the end on behalf of which the whole process takes place. Finding no such end, he calls his education 'irrelevant'. What he is suggesting is simply this – that the university exists to confer an idea of man, of a worthy human fate in a time when such a fate is not easily known. Education is an idea of self-realization, of horizons and limits. The student rightly expects his teachers to have some sense of the same end, or to be busy about remedying the lack. This he claims he cannot find, and the claim is all too often true. This is why it is so urgent that the university enlist those energies – the energies of the majority – that are not now enlisted. Enlist them and invest them in a purpose which might, step by step, from small and immediate goals to larger and more comprehensive ones, gradually define in action a viable idea of man, a ripeness worth having and becoming. What such an idea might be, nobody knows or can guess. But nobody will ever know until we take the first step on a way whose destination can only be known by going it. For individuals or institutions, the way is the same. In Pindar's words: 'Become the thing you are'. Or in Buckminster Fuller's translation, 'Truth is a verb'.

Let me close by setting before you a passage which illustrates better than I could say the kind of cultural leadership to which I would like to see the new university lay claim. The author is John Jay Chapman, and he is describing the sort of practical political effectives of such great radicals as Antigone, Wendell Phillips, William Lloyd Garrison, and Ralph Waldo Emerson:

> The radicals are really always saying the same thing. They do not change; everybody else changes. They are accused of the most incompatible crimes, of egoism and a mania

for power, indifference to the fate of their own cause, fanaticism, triviality, want of humor, buffoonery and irreverence. But they sound a certain note. Hence the great practical power of consistent radicals. To all appearance nobody follows them, yet everyone believes them. They hold a tuning-fork and sound A, and everybody knows it really is A, though the time-honored pitch is G flat. The community cannot get that A out of its head. Nothing can prevent an upward tendency in the popular tone so long as the real A is kept sounding. Every now and then the whole town strikes it for a week, and all the bells ring, and then all sinks to suppressed discord and denial.

The reason why we have not, of late years, had strong consistent centers of influence, focuses of steady political power, has been that the community has not developed men who could hold the note. It was only when the note made a temporary concord with some heavy political scheme that the reform leaders could hear it themselves. For the rest of the time it threw the whole civilization out of tune. The terrible clash of interests drowned it. The reformers themselves lost it, and wandered up and down guessing.

It is imagined that nature goes by jumps, and that a whole community can suddenly sing in tune, after it has been caterwauling and murdering the scale for twenty years. The truth is, we ought to thank God when any man or body of men make the discovery that there is such a thing as absolute pitch, or absolute honesty, or absolute personal and intellectual integrity. A few years of this spirit will identify certain men with the fundamental idea that truth is stronger than consequences, and these men will become the most serious force and the only truly political force in their community. Their ambition is illimitable, for you cannot set bounds to personal influence. But it is an ambition that cannot be abused. A departure from their own course will ruin any other of them in a night, and undo twenty years of service.[1]

---

[1] *Practical Agitation*, pages 63–65.

GORDON PARKS

Creativity to me

GORDON PARKS *was born in deep poverty—one of 15 children of a Kansas 'dirt farmer' and a strong-willed mother. To her youngest child, Gordon, when he was 14, she said: 'Let Cherokee Flats be your learning tree.' In 1925 that Kansas town was crude and segregated, but colorful.*

Parks was born on a farm near Fort Scott, Kansas. At age 16 he went to St. Paul to live with an older sister. He had a variety of jobs until 1937 when photography became his obsession. This career gave him experience with the Office of War Information and other government agencies.

He was a Standard Oil photographer for five years until 1949 when he joined Life Magazine, becoming one of the world's highest regarded photo journalists.

Although 'The Learning Tree' is his first effort as a film director, Parks has directed several short films. He wrote the screenplay which was based on his autobiographical novel. He also composed the musical score and three-movement symphony which was recorded by the Munich Symphony Orchestra in 1968.

In 1967, he was voted, in 53 countries, the photographer-writer who has done the most to promote understanding among the nations of the world. That award was presented by the makers of the Nikon cameras, in Japan.

A book of poetry, along with some of his most famous color photographs, was published in 1968, entitled 'A Poet and His Camera.' Currently, he is writing a new novel, 'outside of myself', he says.

Parks claims he works only 75 per cent of his total capacity. I' think anyone who works at 75 per cent of total capability, if talented, can be successful.'

'I've taken only one vacation in my life', Parks says, noting, 'I stayed home and wrote music.'

The more I think about creativity the more I realized how little I know about it. I am not being overly modest. It is just a frank admission that in preparing myself for this discussion, I found that I had an awful lot to be modest about. And in the course of reexamining my early experiences, I began to realize how important they were to whatever I have tried to accomplish.

F. Scott Fitzgerald once wrote that 'we have two or three great and moving experiences in our lives – experiences so great and moving that it doesn't seem at the time that anyone else has been caught up and pounded and dazzled and astonished and beaten and broken and rescued and illuminated and rewarded and humbled in just that way ever before.'

'Then we learn our trade, well or less well, and we tell out two or three stories – each time in a new disguise – Maybe ten times, maybe a hundred, as long as people will listen.... Whether it's something that happened twenty years ago or only yesterday, I must start out with an emotion – one that's close to me and that I can understand.'

I would like to push Fitzgerald's philosophy further, to the need of man simply to dream. To dream remarkable and impossible dreams and to have the desire to fulfil those dreams.

I was about seven when a peculiar fantasy kindled my love for music. The Kansas day was hot, and I was hunting june bugs in our cornfield when I heard a murmuring in the cornstalks. The murmuring grew into music, and I stood there, my mouth full of mulberries, puzzled, looking up at the slow-drifting clouds – wondering if they were the music's source. The violins, horns and drums were as true to me as the sunlight, and I had a feeling that the music was trapped inside my head, that it would be there even if I had no ears. I covered them with my hands, and the sounds were still there and they continued until all the clouds moved away and there was nothing but pale sky. Then it was gone as mysteriously as it had come, and I ran toward the house a little frightened, a little joyful. Then in a frenzy I started banging on our old kimball upright, trying to reproduce the sounds I had heard. My father came in from another part of the field and stood for a moment watching me with astonishment. Later that night he told my mother that he thought her youngest child was going batty.

  I cannot explain this beautiful daydream, other than that it gave me the initial desire to compose music. But in Venice some thirty odd years later, when I sat petrified in the court-yard of the Doges' palace, listening to a large symphony orchestra perform my first piano concerto, I realized that the performance recalled the deprivation, heartbreak, violence, starvation, prejudice, discrimination and love I had come to know since that childhood fantasy back in Kansas. Now, in a sense, this introduces the trials of learning. I had not had a chance for a formal education, so if I were to grapple with that fantasy I had to figure out how I could grapple with the physical situation that confronted me; in other words, how to put notes down on a piece of paper without having had formal musical training. So, I gave each note a number and by playing the numbers consecutively I was able to recall my theme. Now, you might say that it would have been much easier for me to have gone on and studied music, but there was no money. And there were 15 children, so I had to learn how to put those notes together in my own crude way. I did not wait. Had I waited, I do not think that I would have made it to the Festival in Venice with my piano concerto 30 years later.

  For me poetry, photography writing and film-making produce the same mixture of memories. Music comes to my mind as the foremost example because it is the most difficult. I am more in awe of it and more respectful of it as a truly creative process. It defies me. It beats me, breaks me, and rewards me. It lurks in dark corners, dangling elusive notes and themes before me, challenging me to grab hold of what seems like nothing and mold it into something concrete.

I am often asked why I do so many different things. I used to wonder about this myself, and for a long time I passed it off as a sort of professional restlessness. But, in retrospect, I know that it was a desperate search for security within a society that held me inferior simply because I was black. It was a constant inner rebellion against failure. I was a poor black boy who wanted to be somebody. So I created desires until I was drowning neck deep in them, before I would attempt to swim my way out. It was all the more difficult because I was not technically prepared. Two months before I was to be graduated from High School, the great depression of the thirties, plus a physical breakdown, forced me to quit school. Penniless, and without a place to live, I struck out, unprepared and frightened, praying to God for help in one breath, questioning and damning Him in the very next, feeling that He alone was responsible for my predicament.

From then on, everything I touched was used for survival. Basketball, football and photography – simple pleasures for other boys of my age, had to make money for me. In my fright, I set up all sorts of hypothetical tragedies for myself, then I would contemplate an alternative to offset whatever tragedy I felt might strike. For instance, I would imagine I had lost my legs in an accident. Then, just as quickly I would daydream myself into a situation whereby I would play music or perhaps compose for a living. Or if I lost my sight or hearing I could learn Braille and somehow survive by writing. To top it all I had become quite skilled as a cook and dishwasher. (Just last week, when life seemed for a moment to be particularly difficult, I comforted myself with the thought that I could always be a short-order cook.) So with all the tragic possibilities considered, and all the alternatives accounted for, I could push on with a little less fear.

Perhaps if I had been fortunate enough to have gone on to college, to study medicine, engineering or whatever, I would not have become involved in so many other things. More than likely I would have given all my time to one chosen avocation. As it happened I tried several fields. If case one failed me I could turn to another one. Finally, it means that I was forced to rid myself of the insecurities that the lack of education brought me. But, in retrospect, I honestly say that I enjoyed the uncertainty of the broader and more precarious adventure.

So, in Fitzgerald's terms, I go on attempting to reveal my experiences, each time in a different way, through a different medium, hoping that, in some small way, they might make a dent – some mark – on our times. If only I could feel that a photograph, a piece of music or a film of mine could help put an end to hatred, poverty, bigotry or way, the pain of those early years would have been worth while.

Each year scores of young people come to New York asking for advice about entering the field of photography or journalism. I always tell them that they must excel, that something about their work must stand out from those of others. There is, I feel, a logical pattern one must follow to excel. One must learn his craft well – so well that it becomes a natural extension of himself. Second, he must use that craft constantly, finding new ways in which to utilize it. This brings us to the most important aspect of the pattern, that of experimentation. Through it one begins to discover the unpredictable things about his particular craft. And these are the things, hiding, waiting to be flushed out and exposed, that make the difference. One must resist the easy way out, the weakness to settle for what is just acceptable. For many years now I have made it a policy to work beyond the safety limits in photography – just this side of failure with my exposure, disobeying the rules, denying those properly adjusted little cells in my light meter their right to tell me how to expose my film. If

Eastman Kodak cautions not to shoot into the sun, I shoot into the sun. If they say, do not use indoor film outdoors, I disobey to try for an unusual result. When I should be expected to hold my camera steady, there is something rebellious in me that says, twirl it. And I did just that on a story in which I was attempting to capture the difficult philosophy of the renowned Jesuit priest, Teilhard de Chardin. And, fortunately, the result was worth it.

So, as I become professionally comfortable in a certain field, I begin to search for a new challenge in that field. The late Vivian Rivkin, who performed three of my piano sonatas, used to threaten to slit my throat because I insisted that she strike a particular cluster of notes with her fist instead of in a more pianistic way, with her fingers. She told me: 'I would not dare do that before an audience'. I worked with her for one full afternoon on this passage, which was a rather violent one. Finally, after pounding her fingers swollen trying to gain the effect, she shouted, 'to hell with that stupid chord!' And she banged it with her fist. And to her chagrin, and my pleasure, she banged it the same way during the concert that evening.

In the shooting of my first major film, 'The Learning Tree', I was not so comfortable; maybe the million or so it cost had something to do with my being less adventurous. It is infinitely more difficult to achieve a direct creative expression with a motion picture camera than it is with a still camera. Between me and that lens, that exposure, was a cameraman (who does not himself work the camera) and his operator. On *The Learning Tree* I once looked up to see a patch of birds flying by, a beautiful sight. 'Bernie, Bernie, look at that' 'I said to the cameraman, and he said, 'Yeah, beautiful, huh?' I stood there and watched the birds fly out of sight, frustrated to realize we could not just lift up that huge camera and shoot.

There is a loss, even when you have a great cameraman like Bernie Guffey. In music I am in complete control. In writing a novel, outside of an argument with my editor, I am in complete control. In writing poetry, I am in complete control, but in films you work through and with others, including several people upstairs who are going to control the money all the way. I was very fortunate in having a young man by the name of Kenneth Heyman who gave me all the freedom that I needed for my first film. So whatever there was about that film that you liked or disliked is my responsibility. Heyman asked me to adapt *The learning tree* for the film because I wrote the novel and when I wrote the theme for the music, Heyman suggested that I write the whole score, which I did. Then it was decided that I should produce it if I wanted to keep control. So now I am the first black director in Hollywood, another one of those firsts that you get a little tired of because there should not be that 'first black' all the time. People think possibly that you are proud of it – you are not really. We should have had black directors years ago. Maybe the Indians would have won more often if we had.

But by the time my second film comes around I hope to have the courage to use the camera more daringly. It would have been foolish for me to strike out wildly before getting my medium well in hand. It would have been like some painters I know, who jumped into abstraction without first learning to become good draftsmen. Abstract form can be extremely detrimental to a composer who has not been trained in the fundamentals of composition. Or to a poet who ignores the importance of metre. How often have I heard the phrase, 'Man, that's wild!'. Wild is beautiful when it is tempered with intelligence and good taste. Wild just to be wild is not the thing. And, it helps an awful lot if you know something about what you are trying to be wild about.

There is something else one needs besides a command of one's craft. I would like to explain this by recalling two essays I did on poverty for *Life* magazine. One was on Flavio, a small boy I found dying in the Favela above Rio de Janeiro, and another on the Fontenelle family in the slums of Harlem. The first and most important things I had to create in either essay was friendship – a sincere bond. And in both cases understanding was more important than technical skill. The understanding of hunger, sickness and death on an unbearably hot mountainside; the understanding of hunger, violence and death in the bitter cold of a northern ghetto. In fact, I spent the first three days with the Fontenelles without once taking out my camera. The time was much better spent involving myself in their immediate problems, getting to know them, getting them to know me – so that they would accept me. For, in a journalistic sense, I needed them more than they needed me. The act of sharing confidences had to be made before they, or I, could let the camera intrude on their privacy without a certain amount of embarassment. Not until I was sure that they felt easy when I was around did I start to shoot. And during the three months I spent with them, I saw situations I would have liked to have photographed, but did not, because there are certain intimacies into which I feel the camera should not intrude. Sure, I lost an important picture or two, but I valued a thousand times more the friendship they gave me for honoring moments which they preferred not to share with the outside world.

Now, I remember that after I began the piece on the slum child in Rio de Janeiro I became so involved in Flavio and his family and that hill, that I forgot that I had come to Brazil to do a story. I forgot *Life* Magazine altogether and disappeared. *Life* felt that something had happened to me and they sent people out to look for me in the hills because the territory was very dangerous. Several people had been killed in that area trying to take pictures. By this time I had left my hotel on the sumptuous beach down below. I lived there with that family for a period of three weeks in one little shack where altogether about 12 or 13 of us slept, and ate red beans and rice and stale bread and coffee. To report that story honestly I had to thoroughly share the experience with those people. But I knew that at any minute I could walk out of it. The tragic thing was that they were doomed there forever and that although I was bringing little Flavio out – which eventually I did – I was leaving tens of thousand of people behind. So you say, 'Well what good did you do?'. The good, I think was that millions were made aware of what poverty was really like in Brazil; and I embarassed the Brazilian government to the extent that they are now trying to do away with the Favelas. That was my same purpose in Harlem, to try to get our government to eliminate the Favelas or the Barrios or the ghettos of our communities. Unfortunately I have not been quite so successful as I was in Brazil.

And there were times, several of them, when with Flavio and his family, I had to drop the camera and physically intervene to prevent a disaster. One such instance was when the boy's younger sister became angry with him and attempted to plunge a knife into his back. Instinctively I went for her poised wrist with my right hand. I underestimated her strength, for she jerked loose for another attempt. There was nothing to do but to drop my camera and restrain her with both my hands. The next moment she was crying – begging me for money, seemingly unaware that she had just threatened the life of her brother.

There was a tremendous public response to both stories. And with the public's financial help I was able to bring Flavio to America, where he was cured, and to buy his family a nice home miles from the dreaded Favela. Similarly, the Fontenelles escaped their ghetto through public generosity and substantial help through *Life* magazine. I cannot help but feel that these were two of my most successful stories. I mention them to point up the fact that creativity, in a literal sense, is not always the primary function of a successful photographic story. It is sometimes subservient to another kind of ability, one that has to do with man's response to man – one that has more to do with the human spirit.

Less than two weeks ago I went to Algeria for a two-day meeting with Eldridge Cleaver. It was the first time I met him. I found him astonishingly bright, uncompromising and refreshingly honest. He tells me he is coming back to this country. If he does, I honestly think he is returning to certain death. Because it seems that those who sent him into political exile want him dead. Still, he says that he is coming back, to avoid another kind of death – the death inside, which to a man of his creative force, is as bad as the other kind of death. As I left him for the last time on a wet windswept street, I could not help but damn the tragedy of this brilliant young man, a man who found himself while behind prison walls, and emerged one of the most creative writers of our time. But those who sent him scurrying into exile on a trumped-up charge would hardly know about creativity. They give him more trouble now than when he was a robber.

I am afraid you have to be black to really understand Eldridge Cleaver – and a special kind of black at that. I understand him because when I was his age I had every reason to hate every white man I saw, because of the ill treatment he had heaped upon me. It was time to fight back. There was the knife, the club and there was the gun – and there were the as yet untapped resources that lay deep inside me. I chose to gamble on myself rather than on the weapons. The choice was not entirely deliberate, for I had been brought up to abhor violence and to respect my fellow man. Up to now, I have never been sorry for that choice. I am trying to keep the faith, brother Agnew and brother Nixon – trying to keep the faith.

The thousands of letters that come to me is reasonable evidence that I have communicated. These letters help me to keep faith in people – and in myself. So, I suppose, they are the rewards I honor most; having found their way through the rubble of fear and human deprivation with a six-cent stamp and a message inside that says, *brother, I dig you.*

We cannot be proud of what we did in the decade just finished, what with assassinations, civil violence and war. True, the moon landing was a spectacular, creative achievement. If only we could somehow turn some of that awesome creativity inward, to serve the human heart, then one could be more optimistic about the decade ahead. We must not make the error of limiting the use of creative talents. Words, images and music are in abundance. Placed end to end they could make a path a million times to the moon. But we grow weary of words – because they have grown hollow. We tired to the music of unfilled promises. And we have grown to distrust the images that our present society molds for us. Somehow, in some way, we must bring new meaning to creativity. We must use it fully and in the broadest sense, if we are to inspire men to real brotherhood and a lasting peace.

Columbia College Library
Columbia, Missouri

DATE DUE

OCT 25 74			
NOV 8 74			
NOV 22 74			
SEP 18 75			
APR 17 72			
MAY 11 84			
APR 27 87			
JUL 16 1997			
Reserve			
Sun 98			
Christy			

GAYLORD — PRINTED IN U.S.A.